Singing in the Fire

Singing in the Fire

Stories of Women in Philosophy

Edited by
Linda Martín Alcoff

ROWMAN & LITTLEFIELD PUBLISHERS, INC.
Lanham • Boulder • New York • Oxford

ROWMAN & LITTLEFIELD PUBLISHERS, INC.

Published in the United States of America
by Rowman & Littlefield Publishers, Inc.
A Member of the Rowman & Littlefield Publishing Group
4501 Forbes Boulevard, Suite 200, Lanham, Maryland 20706
www.rowmanlittlefield.com

P.O. Box 317
Oxford
OX2 9RU, U.K.

British Library Cataloguing in Publication Information Available

Library of Congress Cataloging-in-Publication Data

Singing in the fire : stories of women in philosophy / edited by Linda
Martín Alcoff.
p. cm.
Includes bibliographical references and index.
ISBN 0-7425-1382-3 (alk. paper) — ISBN 0-7425-1383-1 (pbk. : alk. paper)
1. Women philosophers. I. Alcoff, Linda.
B105.W6S56 2003
108'.2—dc21 2003002144

Printed in the United States of America

∞™ The paper used in this publication meets the minimum requirements of American National Standard for Information Sciences—Permanence of Paper for Printed Library Materials, ANSI/NISO Z39.48-1992.

For Vrinda Dalmiya and Elizabeth Potter,
my own personal suppliers of asbestos.

Contents

Acknowledgments

This book has caused in me a kind of anguish even beyond the usual anguish I feel in publishing, due to worries about both its likely political and its personal effects on our discipline as well as on our lives. I leaned on many people for help. The authors included herein inspired me with their courage and taught me many things in our exchanges, things about philosophy, about life, and about the intersection of the two. Many other women in philosophy also gave me help, encouragement, and sound advice, including Vrinda Dalmiya, Iris Young, Lynne McFall, Linda Bell, and Peg Simons. At a moment's notice, Libby Potter read through the introduction and helped me to think through issues of tone as well as substance. Eve DeVaro from Rowman & Littlefield was very supportive and helpful throughout. George Yancy, who has edited two recent books of autobiographical essays by philosophers, was also critically helpful in his encouragement and his concrete suggestions from the beginning.

Yancy's volumes, one on African American philosophers and one that is a more general collection, provided a model for my own. (I am constrained from saying that his volumes are wonderful because I am in one of them, but they really are wonderful: quite well-done and very interesting.) But Sara Ruddick's collection *Working It Out: 23 Women Writers, Artists, Scientists, and Scholars Talk about Their Lives and Work*, which she edited with Pamela Daniels over twenty years ago, was the inspiration for the idea of this book. The themes that organized Sara's book might be taken from the chapter on "The Independent Woman" in Simone de Beauvoir's *Second Sex*, that is, the challenges faced by women when we pursue intellectual work. These challenges include male-dominated styles of work and male-centered organizations of the workplace but also the obstacle that feminine socialization becomes when we pursue any individual, non-family-related project. I know from discussing that book with so many women that reading such personal, literary, and confessional (before that became a dirty word) stories written by such fascinating and successful women made us all feel less weird and crazy for having so many internal monologues of doubt, and then having monologues about our monologues! *Working It Out* gave us, as consciousness-raising at its best had done, a political context for our difficulties but without the abstractions of structural analysis or the objective distancing of social psychology. Besides inspiring the current book, Sara was enormously generous in lending her help with many aspects of the editing process over several months. I am deeply in her debt.

Introduction

Linda Martín Alcoff

In the last century, women went from having a complete absence among professional philosophers in the United States to achieving a representation that is now nearing 20 percent. From being denied entry into many colleges and universities, even as undergraduate students, even up until the 1970s, some of us have now become full professors in graduate departments. How did this change occur? How were those who were the first women in their Ph.D. programs treated by students and faculty? And how did they survive?

This collection of autobiographical essays will begin to answer these questions. Included here are first-person accounts from many of the pioneers of our profession—women who entered philosophy departments at a time when in most there had never been a woman professor, much less a woman president of the American Philosophical Association (APA), and when philosophy written by women was all but invisible. The women included here not only stayed; they succeeded to become respected and influential.

The stories collected here explain how the authors survived a socialization into mid-twentieth-century femininity with their intellects, and their intellectual curiosity, intact. These stories also explain how the authors negotiated, sometimes accepting and sometimes resisting, the standard second-class treatment of female graduate students, and how they worked around the restrictions imposed on women, especially mothers, in the workplace. Readers will also get a sense of the development of feminist philosophy from its first amorphous emergence, and its early links to critical social theory as well as the anti-imperialism of the antiwar movement. The stories collected here provide a rich and diverse sample, with no political uniformity among the authors beyond the commitment to work toward more justice for women—however they define that idea.

These women are all brilliant, complex, and philosophically astute, with sufficient experience in the profession to consider with maturity and measure how they have been treated, how they might have done things differently, and how we might be able to make some progress for the next generation. Indeed, there are two past presidents of the APA represented here, as well as elected members of the APA Divisional Executive Committees, leaders of other academic organizations, and women who have led philosophy toward whole new arenas of philosophical work.

Philosophy is a demanding and extremely competitive discipline. For several decades now, the job market has been so difficult that I have heard more than one APA president say a person must be slightly crazy to pursue a career in philosophy. However, women have faced special challenges, and often the price of our survival in the profession has been our silence. I remember well that in the spring term of the first year of my master's degree program, I discovered I was pregnant, this despite the aggressive use of contraception. My husband and I, both in shock, debated the pros and cons of continuing the pregnancy, given that he had just been laid off work, that we were without health insurance, that we had a two-year-old child already, and that I had just won a small scholarship for the following year. During this period of uncertainty, I did not want to tell my professors of my condition, and I was especially concerned not to reveal my morning sickness in my 10 A.M. class on "Augustine and Aquinas," where the professor was a young Thomist with a wife who cared for their six children at home. Thus, I struggled to maintain my head in a fixed and stable position throughout the morning classes, even while I felt I must have been turning green and had to fight an overwhelming temptation to slide out of my chair and onto the floor. I participated in a university-sponsored public debate later that year on the question of abortion. I argued in favor of its remaining a legally protected practice whereas my opponent argued in favor of making it illegal. Here again, I chose to keep silent about the fact that I had had an abortion at the age of sixteen, which gave me insight into the philosophical issues on the topic but which also made it emotionally taxing for me to engage in public debates, even in seminars.[1] Some years later, I had to ask a professor for an incomplete grade in a graduate seminar because my children had had consecutive bouts of chicken pox, thus requiring me to miss two full weeks of class. He was fully sympathetic, but he instructed me to lie on the form about the reason for my request, explaining that if certain parties found out that my family responsibilities had interfered with my course work, they would simply say I had no business pursuing a Ph.D. Shortly after I became an assistant professor, I was loudly called a "bush" by a senior colleague in front of graduate students (in the departmental office!), though what he said to me in the privacy of my own office was even more disconcerting. Another (female) colleague convinced me to speak to my chair about it, yet the person never desisted; and so, I ultimately had to find ways to avoid or endure his persistent provocations on my own.

Overt and explicit forms of sexual harassment, which can cause a lot of stress and even the loss of jobs or degrees, have received recent public attention (although philosophers as a group generally seem seriously behind the rest of the academy in their understanding about what counts as harassment and why it is wrong). But women in the academy face many more kinds of challenges than sexual harassment, from having to keep pregnancies secret to having to keep one's child-care responsibilities invisible and to a minimum (while men sometimes receive admiration for attending to their family responsibilities) to foregoing children and even partners altogether. In addition, a persistent tradition of sexism from colleagues, administrators, and students (both male and female) subtly demeans our capacities, undermines our confidence, and undercuts our ability to perform at our best. Perhaps worst of all, publication, hiring, salary, and promotion decisions have been affected in demonstrable ways in some cases by sexist prejudice.[2] I have heard male faculty suggest that a female faculty member got pregnant just so that she could get a research leave. I was shocked to hear a male philosopher I know comment about a prominent female philosopher that "I don't know if she would have even been in philosophy except for her husband." Senior women who ask for the same things that senior men ask for are often called "divas," a term with no male equivalent. Prominent women who have a following of graduate students and younger philosophers are called "queen bees," even though men with comparable influence are simply admired.

In the not-too-distant past, it was quite routine to deny women graduate fellowships on the grounds that it was a "waste" to give them to women. Women with Ph.D.'s, even from leading departments, were never considered worthy of tenure-track positions but were instead hired only as instructors or adjuncts. Women seeking jobs were asked regularly about their relationships and their plans to have children. This was the climate of the profession when many of the contributors to this volume were beginning their careers. One still finds ugly rumormongering about senior women's sex lives that is clearly based on antiquated double standards as well as great leaps of inference that we instruct our logic students against. Sometimes our esteemed profession seems little different from high school, where sexual rumors about girls are used to isolate and demean them and where the normative male and female roles are exhaustively represented by the metaphor of football players and cheerleaders.

Today such statements may well be castigated as manifestations of the "culture of complaint," which suggests that anyone who can claim victim status happily does so and proceeds to whine with an attitude of self-righteous martyrdom. More than one of the women included in this volume have schooled themselves to avoid complaining at all cost, even in the face of outrageous indignities, and they found the task of telling the simple truth about their lives as women in philosophy a daunting proposition, given the likelihood they would be seen as "whiners." But as philosophers, we clearly need to make some distinctions here.

We all know whiners on the job, the people who complain but do nothing to address the problems they are complaining about; who blame others while never considering their own faults; who seem too wedded to their self-image as the unjustly treated; and who cannot seem to distinguish between petty aggravations and serious problems. Obviously, however, every complaint of unfair treatment is not an example of such whining. In fact, many of those women who do have the courage to complain and even to attempt remedial action about very serious problems in the academy are vilified not just as whiners but as hysterics, whores, and/or general incompetents. This suggests that what we have is less a culture of complaint and more a culture of cruelty toward anyone who challenges male privilege. If members of the philosophy profession refuse to hear or consider clear statements about the problems in our discipline, then they are simply operating as apologists for an unjust status quo.

Women's experiences in philosophy have not all been difficult, of course, and they have steadily improved. My experience is probably typical in that as an undergraduate in the 1970s, I had no female philosophy professors, nor were there female philosophy teaching assistants or graduate students at my university. As an M.A. student in the early 1980s, I had one female philosophy professor, Linda Bell, and I also had the opportunity to take one of the first courses on feminist issues in philosophy, which she had courageously developed. In my Ph.D. program, there were two female professors at the associate level and about 20 to 25 percent of the graduate students were women. Today, most departments would probably feel remiss if they did not have a single woman on the faculty. European American women have especially made significant strides; the scant numbers of women of color is in line with the dismal limitations of the profession as a whole (African American men and women comprise less than 5 percent of the profession; Latinas and Latinos make up less than 2 percent; and Asian Americans and American Indians fare even worse).[3] We must surely acknowledge that those of us who have obtained tenure are extremely fortunate, after all, with better and more secure jobs than the majority of workers, even in rich societies. Women's enjoyment is no doubt all the sweeter, for we are all aware how close we came—just one generation—to being unable in all likelihood to practice philosophy. But the writers collected here were brave enough to express their range of experiences, positive and negative. My hope is that the analysis of discrimination given especially by respected senior European American women will help push open the door wider than it currently is, making it possible for more women of color to enter.

My intent was precisely to collect the stories of women who are generally over fifty and thus senior enough to have seen some significant changes in the academy. I was loose with the age limit to try to ensure some ethnic diversity, though there is unfortunately too little (see the essays by Narayan and Schutte).[4] Women at this level have many demands on their time and stacks of prior commitments. Most of those whom I invited were supportive of the project, but some understandably had to decline. It is interesting that quite a few were unwilling out of a concern for the repercussions they may face if they "told the truth," a consequence that can be quite unpleasant even for those with tenure and stature. Beyond specific recriminations, there can be a general disapproval of female scholars for making personal revelations of any sort: it can lessen our collective, hard-won credibility; invite accusations of personal exhibitionism; or reinforce the tendency to view our gender identity as all-determining over our thought, life, and work. Why take such risks? For the simple reason that true examples have a greater impact than any arcane thought experiments in altering people's beliefs about the world.

Some years ago a woman colleague, Lynne McFall, and I decided, with no doubt the foolhardiness of the naïve and untenured, to do an anonymous survey of all the women connected with our department—faculty, graduate students, and office workers—about the conditions of their work in general and about any problems of sexual harassment they experienced in particular. We were motivated by some particular and persistent problems, but our intention in doing the survey was decidedly not to point fingers at individuals nor to establish evidence; rather, it was to try to generate a general conversation about the conditions for women in our department. We planned to collect the surveys and write a report that would provide a picture of the current conditions and problems without specific information regarding individuals. This objective may seem hardly possible, but I believe we managed to pull off the anonymity, which was proven by the fact that some male faculty members were desperate to know "who" had done *x*, *y*, or *z* as described in our report. They did not want to have an open and general discussion of problems for women in the department; they just wanted to know who was culpable and whether they were personally on that list. Lynne and I were very frustrated by this reaction. It indicated a great deal of concern for self-protection with little or no concern for whether the women were being treated with fairness and respect.

Litigation, of course, requires establishment of clear culpability, though culpability can sometimes accrue to groups or institutions and not just individuals. But litigation is not the only nor is it always the best remedy for certain kinds of problems. In writing up our survey, we thought that many men lacked information on *(a)* what commonly occurs to women and *(b)* how these occurrences generally affect women. We hoped they would be interested to learn about the reality of women's lives in our department and thus be motivated to develop remedies.

This book is another attempt to provoke a general conversation.

Some themes here may not seem related to gender at all, but I urge readers to consider whether what may look like universal problems are really unrelated to gender. Consider the following themes that appear in these essays: the theme of finding a way to make philosophy "meaningful," or "relevant" as we used to say in the 1960s, has been especially important for many women who have found themselves incapable of ignoring the world around them; the theme of finding a way to have a private life as well as a professional one, which can be a challenge for men as well but not generally as great a challenge as women still face; and the theme of lack of confidence. I remember being totally amazed when a senior woman whom I admired and considered brilliant shared with me how constant her lack of confidence has been throughout her career. (The woman was Sandra Bartky, and in her essay here, she writes with great wit and humor about her struggles of confidence). But then I remembered a woman my mother worked with who said that in professional life, a woman had to be like a duck: smooth on the surface and paddling like hell underneath. We enter these previously male-only realms and try hard to maintain our sense that we have a right to be here, but as Simone de Beauvoir described so clearly fifty years ago, the heightened self-consciousness that is inevitable when crossing a social barrier interferes with focused concentration and the easy confidence of presumed entitlement.[5] As I now tell younger women who struggle with giving conference papers, what you need is a good bluff. You cannot conquer the confidence problem just as an act of willpower, but you can develop a placid demeanor and a confident expression. One never can tell how many of the women perusing the meetings of the APA with confident expressions are in actuality paddling like hell underneath.

Academic philosophy in the APA feels today sometimes like a case of parallel worlds. In one, white men in suits, or at least in sports jackets, congregate in large halls at the conventions, filling the sessions, and dominating all the research departments and most others besides. The tone of speakers is serious, sometimes arrogant, often clever, and devoid of personal or cultural reference. But today there is a parallel world to this older one, a world that is much newer, much smaller, but vigorous and growing. This world is not quite the polar opposite of the first world, as in Star Trek, where the good Kirk and Spock must fight the evil Kirk and Spock. In this case, Uhuru's at the helm, Spock is a yeoman, and Kirk is apparently absent.

Of course, the thought of African American women having control over philosophy is at this stage pure fantasy; however, what does exist is a feeling of parallel worlds in the sense that there are now two arenas of philosophical work that currently have, alas, too little intersection. All of us must have some presence in that first world, or we cannot survive in the profession. But reciprocal interest and participation in the second world remains small. In this latter world, new philosophical questions are emerging that have never been asked before in academic halls.

Women today are often operating in both worlds with vigor, if not with great representation. This book is also an effort to represent a diversity of women who operate in different ways in the field: some who are leading insiders to the APA, others who purposefully avoid the APA; some who are stalwarts of the Society for Women in Philosophy (SWIP)—a major player in the parallel world—and others who are not primarily involved in feminist philosophy or SWIP and who in fact may be quite critical of them.

In order to improve the situation of women in philosophy further, we need to begin to share criticisms and disagreements concerning both our organizational work and our philosophical ideas. Neither will advance without critique, although I continue to agree with the many feminists who believe that there is more than one way to do critique and that the adversary method so persuasively analyzed by Janice Moulton is neither necessary nor always the best means to advance philosophical truth.[6] Still, all of us need to fight our small-group mentality or our prejudgements, and hear from women across the discipline. I myself have never been content with what we on the left refer to as "small-group politics," in which the politically marginalized come to revel in their marginal status and forget organizing rule number one: get in there with the masses and struggle. I do not at all mean to imply that problems occur only or more so among some arenas and less in others. The problem of insularity happens on all fronts, from women who are so identified with certain trends that they dismiss those who act or think differently, to women who still fear being tarred with low status if they are seen to fraternize *[sic]* too much with the girls instead of the boys. I think most or all of us, certainly I, have probably made mistakes in both of these regards. Women of all political orientations who are concerned about women's situation in the profession need to listen to all the women's stories and diverse analyses.

Women in philosophy will no doubt always disagree with one another (we are, after all, philosophers). Yet I would argue that the difficulties among women in our profession need to be analyzed in a political context. In brief, the less powerful and less secure groups in any constituency are easily divided and often more desperately competitive. Moreover, women as a group are hardly immune from the heterosexism and racism widespread in our society, and some can be fearful of being perceived as lesbian or can be peremptorily dismissive of the claims of people from other ethnic or cultural groups. Sometimes, even feminists themselves fall into either making assumptions about women's sexual opportunism or castigating those who have achieved prestige as necessarily having been morally compromised in order to attain it.

Thus, there is unfortunately plenty of blame to go around. Too many men in power evidence no intention of critiquing the arbitrary aspects of the system that put them there, much less sharing that power. Women of the older generation sometimes forget, or deny, that it took a women's movement for them to be where they are, preferring to believe in their own invincible individual intellect. In addition, women of the younger generation sometimes imagine their senior women mentors to have unrealistic amounts of power, unlimited energy, and the moral duty to support without question all female students. Men who do not have the prestige they imagine they should sometimes scapegoat the women and people of color now in the profession, as if we have personally undermined their careers. And there are still many of both sexes who make negative assumptions about feminist philosophy without having engaged in a serious study of it, in some cases without even having read a single book.

However, I believe strongly that we must fight the cynicism that such persistent problems can sometimes engender. We must expand the unity that we can sometimes find for small projects, in order to push for larger goals, and we must be willing to hear and consider new ideas and uncomfortable viewpoints. Our personal careerism and insecurities too often get in the way of our ability to contextualize the problems we face and to put larger aims than our own at the foremost. I very much admire all of the women who have contributed to this collection for their courage, their honesty, their principled integrity, and their political commitment to advance the situation of women as a whole even at the risk of hurting some of their collegial relationships and diminishing their professional opportunities. Women may not be naturally more moral than men, but I do believe our "outsider within" status in this profession, as in many others, gives rise to a sharp critical eye and can yield a moral compass unrestricted to merely maintaining the internal mechanisms of the discipline.

One contributor who has even more of an "outsider within" status than the rest deserves some special explanation here. I recently was asked by the Pacific division program committee to organize a panel on "being black, gay, Latino/a, female, Asian American, etc. in philosophy before the era of 'diversity.'" At the suggestion of several leading female philosophers who could not come to the panel, I invited Stephanie Lewis to speak to the issue of being female. I did not know very much about Stephanie except in so far as we had had some exchanges in the APA: she serves on the Board of Officers as treasurer of the APA and I had made various appeals to that board in my capacity as chair of the Committee on Hispanics/Latinos. I knew that she had had an "interrupted" career path, having done graduate work at UCLA and Oxford, and that she had been considered good enough to teach as an instructor at several colleges and universities but never offered a tenure-track job. This was of course a very common story for women in the academy in the 1960s and earlier. Moreover, if such women married, as Stephanie had, the consensus of social expectations was that their career aspirations would be subordinated to their husbands' careers, and to caring for their children and maintaining their home lives. In order to understand the "era before diversity," I knew that we needed to hear from a woman who had had that very common experience.

When Stephanie began speaking on that panel, in her characteristically sharp and funny and self-deprecating way, it became immediately clear to all in the room that she was one of the most intelligent people one could ever meet anywhere. Thus the injustice of her exclusion from philosophy was very much the profession's collective loss. To understand the situation in which women attained a foothold in philosophy, we must also take note of the women whose talents the profession squandered. Hence, I entreated Stephanie to write up her comments for this volume, and she, after some long hesitation, complied. I hope she will not regret this decision; I know that readers of this volume will benefit from her contribution to the discussion.

Stephanie entitled her talk on the program and her essay here "Etc." to mark the category that she felt able to represent among those I had listed. From her long tenure in APA leadership, Stephanie contributes a perceptive account of how the profession has made progress toward coming closer to its self-image as a meritocracy.

Why (and how) are women so regularly overlooked, especially in our classrooms? I think we need to engage in a broad discussion about the gendered nature of the intellectual virtues. This area is rich for philosophical work. It involves a whole body of assumptions that are used to assess quality of work and fit characteristics for the academic life. Is temerity and confidence in one's own ideas more important or valuable than receptiveness? Is the problem of being regularly distracted by personal obligations always and only a drag on the philosophical mind, or can it be at least sometimes a resource? Is the ascetic mode of life really the best philosophical model or the best for reaching the truth? Where does love fit into the picture of intellectual virtues, only as interruption and vulnerability or also as perceptive acuity? Obviously, we should not assume that either traditionally masculine or traditionally feminine dispositions are more or less closely aligned with a philosophically inclined intellect, but we do need to take a fresh look at both.

Women often wrestle with these issues, whether or not we have done philosophical work on them, as have Alison Jaggar and Martha Nussbaum, who are included in this volume.[7] We silently wonder if it is our own female proclivities that are keeping us back or if we are in fact just psychologically ill equipped for the academic life. Some of us also daydream about a possible world in which the default image of philosophers would no longer be male. One of the principal ill effects of sexual harassment is its ability to undermine the victim's sense that she has a right to be where she is, doing what she is doing. The motives of the perpetrator of harassment are often to send just such a message.

What has come to be called sexual harassment has been almost a constant across my various jobs and schools, and I am not referring to simple compliments (which some think feminists overblow into harassment) or invitations but clear attempts to put me in my place or to enjoy sexual contact without my consent. A favorite philosophy professor tried to undress me in a hallway when I was an undergraduate, and both my beloved high school physics teacher and, later, my boss in the physics lab where I worked during college took advantage of moments when we were alone to accost me. As I already related, when I was a new assistant professor, I was loudly called a "bush" in front of graduate students by a senior colleague. My chair's promise to "speak to him" seemed to have no effect on his subsequent regular editorial comments. My husband came up with a rather obscene nickname for this guy, for my private amusement and mental health, but when my sons picked it up, I had to be careful to keep them several rooms apart from him during departmental parties. From discussions with other women, these kinds of experiences are certainly on the milder side of what women sometimes get from male philosophers. I was also very fortunate in both my graduate schools to have been treated with consistent respect and to have had several energetic and wonderful male mentors. However, I have twice been a whistle-blower in sexual harassment cases affecting students, and it has cost me dearly.

It was not until my second year of graduate school that I took a course in philosophy with a woman professor: Linda Bell's "Philosophy of Woman" at Georgia State University, where I was working toward an M.A. Her confidence that I could someday move from student to teacher both floored me and solidified my determination. She treated me with real respect, as she did all of her students, and she became a model that showed me a different way to be a philosopher, with all of her care and concern for the world inside (rather than left behind) her philosophical "rigor."[8] The only other female professor that I studied with later in my Ph.D. program was Martha Nussbaum, who was similar to Linda Bell in exemplifying a kind of feminine philosophical form. Rather than aiming toward "out manning" the men, Linda and Martha quietly and confidently went about philosophy in their own way, drawing from their lives (but without privileging their own experience) and insistently bringing philosophy down to earth in both its subject matter and its method. And personally, they were (and are) women with rich lives, lives that included sexuality, political passions, strong familial commitments, and in Martha's case, motherhood. Thus, I was quite privileged to have two such examples of how to be both a woman and a philosopher without inviting internal dissonance.

Within a few weeks of discovering the pregnancy that appeared during my master's program, my husband and I decided to go forward with it. He managed to get a temporary job driving taxis, and I took a second job while accepting the scholarship. With my comprehensive exams approaching, I was determined to finish them before the baby came, knowing from previous experience how much would be demanded of me when I brought the baby home. So I found myself taking my exams at nine-months pregnant, having to stretch out my arms to reach the table for the four-hour exam. Besides the practical motive, I also had in the back of my head a determination to prove that, no matter how busy a woman's body was, her mind could still perform at its peak. I passed the exam, then gave birth three weeks later.

Just two days after Teresa Brennan sent me the final revisions of her essay for this volume, she was hit by a car while crossing the street, went into a coma, and subsequently, in a matter of weeks, passed away at the age of fifty-one. Teresa was a bravely original philosopher, astonishingly erudite, and her own recent work on the transmission of affect—the ways in which we transfer emotional states to one another—has the potential for causing us to rethink assumptions in the metaphysics of the self, the philosophy of mind, as well as political theory. Teresa was intensely feminist in her head, her heart, and her soul (and she was one of the few feminist theorists who openly declared a belief in souls).

She was also a friend and mentor. In the fall of 2000, I spent a semester as a visiting professor in the innovative, interdisciplinary Ph.D. program at Florida Atlantic University that she helped to design and found. For four months I was fortunate to enjoy her company and her intellectual stimulation. One bit of advice she gave me then has had ever since a transfixing effect, as one of those life-altering moments that will affect one forever hence. She asked me, "Have you ever written precisely and exactly what you truly think and believe, without editing yourself down? Have you ever thought about writing not for a present-day audience but for the future?" Teresa's own writing was always like this—direct, fully honest, and with an eye toward the possibilities of a better future for all women.

She is greatly missed.

NOTES

1. I fully acknowledge that the choice to have an abortion can be extremely difficult and painful for men as well, but women experience a live, physical difference that intensifies the feelings of loss and sadness.

2. Some potential contributors to this volume had to decline due to the fact that they are in litigation against their universities for just such grievances. Those who mistakenly believe that "women and minorities" are getting red-carpet treatment in higher education should look at research done by the American Association of University Professors, the American Association of University Women, and the United

University Professors, whose comparative studies of faculty salaries show persistent gender and race discrimination. Many of these issues have also been taken up by the Committee on the Status of Women of the Society for Phenomenology and Existential Philosophy, and the Committee on the Status of Women of the American Philosophical Association. I recommend readers to the APA web page where they can read the reports of its diversity committees (www.apa.udel.edu/apa/). Another good source of information is in the *Newsletter on Feminism and Philosophy*, available through the APA.

3. The APA now has committees and newsletters representing the concerns of each of these groups. Again, I urge readers to consult the committee reports and numerous newsletter articles exploring these problems. These are available on the APA website—see note 2.

4. For more on non–European American women in philosophy, see the interviews with Anita Allen, Michele M. Moody-Adams, Naomi Zack, Angela Davis, Joy James, and Adrian Piper, prominent African American philosophers, in George Yancy's edited collection, *African-American Philosophers: 17 Conversations* (New York: Routledge, 1998).

5. See her *The Second Sex*, translated by H. M. Parshley (New York: Vintage, 1989), especially the chapter "The Independent Woman." Though originally published in 1949, Beauvoir's descriptions have enduring relevance, even across race and class divides in some cases, as my students regularly attest.

6. See Janice Moulton, "The Adversary Method," in *Discovering Reality: Feminist Perspectives on Epistemology, Metaphysics, Methodology, and Philosophy of Science,* edited by Sandra Harding and Merrill B. Hintikka (Dordrecht, Holland: D. Reidel, 1983), 149–64. See also the Symposium in the spring 2001 *Newsletter on Feminism and Philosophy* on "Intra-Feminist Criticism and the 'Rules of Engagement,'" with contributions from Ann Garry, Naomi Zack, Marilyn Frye, Martha Nussbaum, and Naomi Scheman, volume 00, no. 2 (82–97).

7. See Alison M. Jaggar, "Love and Knowledge: Emotion in Feminist Epistemology," in *Gender/Body/Knowledge: Feminist Reconstructions of Being and Knowing*, edited by Susan R. Bordo and Alison M. Jaggar (New Brunswick, N.J.: Rutgers University Press, 1989); and Martha C. Nussbaum, *Love's Knowledge: Essays on Philosophy and Literature* (New York: Oxford University Press, 1990).

8. For Linda Bell's own story, see her forthcoming book *Beyond the Margins: Reflections of a Feminist Philosopher* (Albany, N.Y.: SUNY Press, 2003).

1

A Life Sentence in Bohemia

Sandra Lee Bartky

I entered graduate school in the late 1950s to escape what seemed to loom before me as my fate: a life sentence in some dead-end female job ghetto or worse, 1950s suburban housewifery. Years before the reappearance of feminism, I was already an instinctive marriage resister, but graduate school was a compromise. What I really wanted was to hang out in Greenwich Village or, even better, the Left Bank of the Seine. I never actually saw myself *doing* anything important, indeed, doing anything at all except relishing the ambiance and all the interesting folk. After having been rejected by all the Jewish sororities on campus in my freshman year (in those days, they were all segregated: are they still?), I discovered in my sophomore year where I really belonged: in bohemia. Indeed, a large bohemian crowd was in the midst of my rah-rah, land-grant Midwestern state university. (This all happened so long ago that even beatniks had not yet appeared on the cultural landscape.)

Campus bohemia: a large crowd of aspiring actors, writers, poets, painters, and musicians. There was also a goodly number of eccentrics, poseurs, and pseudointellectuals. I was somewhat haunted during this period by the suspicion (well-founded, in fact) that I was myself a pseudointellectual. At any rate, I was welcomed into this company; indeed, in time I became one of its leading lights. We distinguished ourselves from the Greeks and the straight independents by our dress and appearance: lots of the guys had beards (odd in those Eisenhower days) and berets; we women wore nothing but black turtleneck sweaters, black pants, lots of dark eye makeup, and, in my case, heavy Mexican jewelry. A liberal arts major, I briefly turned my hand to poetry and short stories. This was now my second incarnation, having begun college as a music major.

In those days, we all believed that anything European was better than anything American, from bicycles and movies to bread and the arts. And so, as graduation approached, I began to wonder how I could manage to worship at the shrine of European culture. Things were a lot less competitive for my small depression-era cohort, so I applied for and won a Fulbright scholarship to study philosophy in Germany (even though I had only minored in it). I had no particular desire to go to Germany (although anywhere in Europe would have been wonderful), but one had to first demonstrate "competence" in the language, which was defined as two years of college German (which it certainly *is* not). I believed that every educated person should know (at least) French and German. When, as a music student, I went to register for a language, the line at the French desk was very long. Because I have little patience for waiting in lines of any sort, I registered for German instead, there being no line at all at the German desk. This casual act was to define much of the next fifteen years of my life.

I was in Germany just eleven years after the ending of World War II; most of the major cities, though rebuilding at a very rapid pace, were still surrounded by acres of rubble. I was a Jew. I find it still astonishing that I had then so little historical sense. The war through which I had actually lived, though as a child, was for me but a distant memory, this in spite of the fact that its effects were everywhere to be seen. (This introspection allows me to understand the ahistorical mentalities of most of today's students.) Even though I spent a semester in Munich, I never went to Dachau, even though it was only a trolley ride away. I think that I constructed in my mind and then dwelled in a Germany of Goethe, Heine, and the Brothers Grimm; a Germany that reflected the European fantasy of campus bohemia; a Germany of medieval half-timbered towns, vineyards, sublime ancient churches, and monasteries. Of course, they were there, the cathedrals and monastaries; but it was only in later years, with maturity and some understanding of history that I was able to face what else was there, too.

I set about learning the language. I attended virtually no lectures because I couldn't understand them. I drank. I went dancing almost every night; I had many love affairs. Even on my small stipend, I was able to travel to France, England, Switzerland, Italy, and even Yugoslavia. But over all this gaiety, great art, and good sex hung the dark cloud of guilt. I was taking the government's money (all \$100 per month), but I wasn't studying philosophy! So I began to read philosophy alone in my room, laboriously but tenaciously. Every German philosophy student in those days walked about with a copy of Heidegger's *Sein und Zeit* under his arm so that is what I began to read, too. I was mystified by Heidegger but intrigued as well: his sense of the bleakness of human existence resonated with my own unwavering baseline pessimism about the human condition; this pervasive feeling was always there beneath my fun-loving exterior.

As an undergraduate, I was overjoyed to discover that there was such a thing as graduate school: I could, at least for a while, continue to evade my fate. And if I could get in, they would even pay me to go! Having had no mentoring or advising whatsoever, I didn't know that philosophy departments differed from one another in important ways. So I applied to several, strictly on the basis of the glamour or climate of their location. I was accepted at UCLA. My first and only year there was profoundly unhappy. I longed to be back in Europe. Los Angeles was too big, the people too unfriendly, the smog too unbearable. Worst of all, I discovered the UCLA department to be a nest of positivism. I soon learned that departments did indeed differ from one another, and this one was not for me. I longed to be reading European existential ontology once again, but UCLA was not the place to do it. I applied again to graduate departments and went back to where I had been happy as an undergraduate, the University of Illinois, Urbana-Champaign. (They also offered me a two-year fellowship.) So astonished at my own chutzpah, I set about getting a master's degree, in those days a degree both useful and respectable.

While escape from conventionality was certainly a motive, it was not my only motive. I had, since high school, genuine intellectual interests. But since my high school was so fundamentally anti-intellectual, I never associated anything about the school with the life of the mind, the life I led somewhat surreptitiously at home in my journal. The first philosopher I read in college was Plato, who seemed to offer what young thinkers are looking for—the meaning of existence and a substitute for religion. Plato promised that a true philosopher could become a spectator of all time and all existence. I was hooked. Actually, I had been hooked long before. My father had a very real interest in philosophy, also in mathematics, economics, poetry, criticism, archaeology, and so forth. He was a polymath, an intellectual who had been manipulated into a profession—dentistry—for which he always said he had no aptitude, by an immigrant father who wanted his sons to be successful. My father, born in 1902, had already been practicing dentistry for nearly ten years when the first Jew was appointed to the Harvard faculty. Jews, at least European Jews like us, were not welcome in "complex organizations" such as university faculties and corporations. This discrimination is why so many Jewish men of that generation either started their own businesses or else trained for professions such as law and medicine that they could practice on their own. The women from the immigrant neighborhood where my parents grew up typically did not go to college. They worked until marriage, then, if they had married well, they never worked for wages again. Not having to work for wages was a sign that they had entered the American middle class, that the husband was a good provider, and that she had married well. So the life from which I was fleeing was the very life that announced to the world my mother's success as a woman. My parents loved each other very much. They were friends and partners. He genuinely respected her social and domestic skills, and he was grateful that she had turned him—an introverted, bookish nerd—into a successful social individual. She was grateful that in time (and with his orthodontist's license) he was able to give her a house in the suburbs. But my mother was not an intellectual.

My father, stranded in suburbia, lacked anyone with whom he could share his interests. So he raised me up to be his intellectual companion. He taught me things and told me things. He showed me the structure of the solar system with apples and oranges. Later he shared his philosophical ideas with me as well as his politics. He gave me my first philosophy book, a short history, as well as an introductory psychology text and some of Margaret Mead's anthropological writings. My mother colluded in this: When I would wander into the kitchen and offer to help, she would say, "No, I can do it myself. Go read." So I went and read.

With only a few exceptions, the elderly men (no women) who were my teachers in graduate school had stayed true to their youthful enthusiasms: American pragmatism and process philosophy. The head of the department, D. W. Gotshalk, had been very supportive of me since my undergraduate days. In his own day, he had been an important thinker, producing an ethics, a metaphysics, an epistemology, and an aesthetics. The latter, *Art and the Social Order*, was the most widely read. In temperament, he seemed utterly unlike my father, whose intellectual influence on me had also been very great. Dr. Gotshalk had a serene disposition, and he appeared to be free of all pettiness. He rarely spoke above a whisper. How different from my own household: minor disagreements would turn quickly into shouting and then screaming matches in which everyone's dignity was lost. Mixed into the several motives that impelled me toward philosophy was the desire to emulate the dignity and largeness of spirit I had found in this man. Gotshalk encouraged my interest in phenomenology, which had developed in Germany; knowing little about continental philosophy, he nevertheless let me follow my own daimon, getting an M.A. on the early Heidegger and, in time, a Ph.D. on the later.

It was in graduate school that I was first visited by my own four horsemen of the apocalypse: depression, fear, dread, and panic. Objectively, my career was uneventful: I passed all the Ph.D. prelims the first time (sixteen hours of written material on four consecutive days, followed by a grueling three-hour oral); my grades were mostly A's. Subjectively, I lived much of my life in a low-level panic. One could go through the program in a fairly leisurely way, and because teaching assistants were always needed for Philosophy 101, it was possible for me to spend a year just reading for my prelims. Anticipating this trial, I would from time to time experience a terror so profound it was like a physical seizure. I consciously avoided other graduate students, fearing to reveal the core of stupidity I found within myself. I made friends among the campus poets, musicians, and painters. All that hiding and skulking around corners robbed me of one of the great goods of a graduate education—the casual and playful give-and-take of philosophical discussion, the playing with ideas, the opportunity to match one's wits with others, hence to sharpen them. I was not driven away by my fellow students, all of whom seemed friendly; the sexism from which I suffered was deeper and disguised.

Indeed, I was a victim of "the imposter syndrome," a common affliction among successful women, especially women breaking into formerly male-dominated fields. One feels that one's success is a fluke, that one will be revealed, sooner or later, as a fraud. I discovered many years later, in therapy, that what I lacked, the lack that I feared being exposed, was my lack of a penis! (Of course, one must always be suspicious of "discoveries" made in therapy!) There was another female graduate student in the program, but she kept dropping in and dropping out. I have reason to believe that I am the first woman to be awarded a Ph.D. in philosophy from the University of Illinois.

I was already earning my living teaching philosophy before I met another woman so engaged: this woman was Ruth Marcus, and I was on the search committee that hired her to build a first-rate philosophy program at the new University of Illinois, Chicago (UIC). A telephone call from D. W. Gotshalk had gotten me a job at the two-year ancestor of the present UIC. Jobs were plentiful then, but I had married a man with a business in Chicago and so could not leave. Of the other two persons teaching philosophy there at the time, one did not have a Ph.D. and so could not be on the search committee (I had just been awarded mine), and the other person was himself a candidate.

Ruth Marcus was blissfully free of the anxieties that colored my professional life. As chair of the new department, she surrounded herself with a group of brilliant young philosophers, most of whom went on to earn national reputations. Given her antipathy toward my field, what was regarded as a second-rate Ph.D., and my general air of perpetual apology, I fully expected to be terminated at the end of the year. (She was at that time already an internationally known logician.) But Ruth did not fire me; she gave me the same chance to compete for a position in the new department as the hotshots she was hiring from such places as Harvard and Stanford. Indeed, she became what I had never had before—a mentor. She took me with her to the APA and introduced me to important thinkers. She showed me the importance of being active in the profession. She nudged me into writing philosophical papers. I had no more idea how to do this than had that hapless maiden in the fairy tale whose ambitious father assures the king that his daughter can spin straw into gold. But somehow I did it. She suggested journals where I should send my stuff. In the fullness of time, she supported my tenure; without her support, I doubt I would have gotten it. Of course, during the whole probationary period, I was attended by my own four horsemen, now accompanied by various psychogenic illnesses.

I wonder sometimes why I persisted in spite of such monumental absence of self-esteem. First of all, I think that early on, I learned not to trust entirely my own estimate of myself; I knew enough to let other people determine my merit. A definitive failure would have been a relief; it was the daily struggle against myself that was exhausting. I persisted because I wanted what I thought was the cushy life of a professional academic (summers on the beach) and, as I mentioned earlier, because I was an instinctive marriage resister who saw no other attractive alternative for my life. (How limited was our sense of possibility before the women's movement!) I also wanted the status that went with the job; a base motive, perhaps, but there it was. Finally, I think I persisted because deep down, deep between the layers of my uncomfortable mixture of ambition and terror, lay a genuine love for the subject.

The great social movements of the sixties and seventies—the civil rights movement, the movement against the war in Vietnam, the women's movement, the gay and lesbian movements—changed my life dramatically. They changed my relationship to philosophy, to my society, and to myself. Reaching a certain level of outrage at the cruel and senseless slaughter in Vietnam, I realized that going to demonstrations and writing letters wasn't enough. I needed to get personally involved. So I joined the New University Conference, an organization of progressive young faculty. I soon realized that these people located themselves in the Frankfurt School of Critical Theory; some were openly Marxist. They spoke a language I did not understand, but I found in myself a powerful urge, one that would not be denied, to learn it. And so I retooled. I came to understand my interest in Heidegger much more clearly. The Heideggerian critique of modernity was indeed compelling, but it was presented in a way that was highly mystified, so much so that its effect was, *contra sui*, to support the status quo. As I studied, and in time, began to teach the texts of Marx and other Critical Theorists (such as Marcuse), all sorts of things that had seemed to be disparate phenomena began to come together in a giant synthesis: the vulgarity and materialism of U.S. culture; American imperialism and militarism; the role of ideology not only in pop culture, but in academic discourse as well, even in philosophy; saturation advertising; my own neuroses as responses both to competitive job pressures and to the kind of authoritarian family in which I was raised and in which the system relied at certain times in its development; the presence of abject poverty in the midst of great wealth; the contributions of capitalism to racism and sexism. Things came together for me, the personal as well as the political. While it was clear that I was not to be Plato's "spectator of all time and all existence," I had nevertheless succeeded in making a good deal of sense out of my own society and my place within it; the sense it made, I was to discover, was neither total nor seamless.

When Second Wave feminism appeared in the late sixties, I attached myself to it immediately: as the feminist critique took on flesh, I had another epiphany, similar to what had happened when I encountered Critical Theory. The New University Conference sponsored the first national conference on women's studies, this at a time when there were only two programs in the country, both run largely by students. The idea of women's studies captured my imagination; no one at that early date knew exactly what it would be, but we knew how ignorant we were of women's history and achievements. I spent the next thirty-two years helping to build what is now an outstanding program.

Since the feminist critique of patriarchal society had been for me a revelation and one that overlapped with Critical Theory, it seemed impossible to me that the two could not be brought into some kind of synthesis. I spent the next eight or nine years, along with an emerging group of feminist thinkers, debating the correct ways to think about class, sexual, and racial oppression and the ways to get rid of them. In many ways, this time was the happiest of my life; everything seemed to be coming together: my personal life, my politics, and my philosophical work. All seemed to reflect and support one another. My writing was no longer alienated labor performed unwillingly because my paycheck depended upon it. I became aware much later that we were involved in inventing a world-historical novelty, a new philosophical domain—feminist philosophy. While the hoped-for synthesis never came to pass, this new perspective produced an original philosophical critique of the dominant institutions and discourses, including received versions of both liberalism and Marxism.

I was also deeply involved in organizing women in philosophy to struggle against the deeply rooted prejudice in so many of our colleagues (happily, not all). The small group we were in the beginning grew in time into an international network that now has its own conferences and journals. My own philosophical work was directed toward the clarification of the situation of women like myself (I never thought I could write about all women, everywhere), stressing in particular deeply internalized traits of character and the disciplinary nature of properly "feminine" modes of embodiment. I argued that "femininity" and much that went with it was disempowering to women and that it was presented to women in a highly mystified fashion. My work was therapeutic for many readers, myself included; I used a fundamentally eclectic methodology, joining elements of Critical Theory, analytic philosophy, and phenomenology. I even made some headway against the imposter syndrome, too. I began to understand my internal struggles—a situation that was not the product of any conspiracy—as understandable responses to fear: fear of male hostility toward the female intruder; fear of the loss of femininity with concomitant fear of depersonalization; fear perhaps of competition with my father. My participation in several groups of extremely supportive women was crucial to this development, too. And so, my apocalyptic horsemen galloped away, never to reappear en masse—though I am, from time to time, visited by one or another.

2

My Open Agenda, or How Not to Make the Right Career Moves

Teresa Brennan

Last year, my long-term assistant and collaborator Woden Teachout told a new member of our research team that I was an ambulatory Rorschach blot. Woden was explaining why this intrepid researcher had heard so many contradictory stories about me. "Teresa attracts projections," said Woden. "They tell you about the nature of the person attributing vices or virtues to her."

For some time, various psychoanalytic thinkers have established grounds for linking the phenomenon of projection, splitting good from bad qualities as a matter of human existence, and the endurance of sexism and racism. The process is also called *othering*. In my view, the most enduring manifestation of it lies in the splitting of women into two basic types, passive virgin mother and actively sexual whore. (This split is indissolubly linked to another: good wives and mothers versus bad mothers or stepmothers.) I suggest that this categorical splitting of women is second only to economic disparity as an ongoing cause of sexism. Moreover, while the increasing feminization of poverty fades in and out of middle-class theoretical consciousness, the analysis of stereotypes, particularly those of the mother and the whore, endures from Mary Wollstonecraft through to feminist critiques of role theory and to the more recent analyses of performance in *Fatal Attraction* and *Basic Instinct*. From these horror movies back to Morgan Le Fey (no, at least back to Catallus), the unmarried or insufficiently married woman who enjoys sex is a whore at best and a witch at worst, using her sexual powers to ensnare decent men and have them work her will, casting glamours to mislead the innocent and impressionable.

As the editors' brief for this good idea (women philosophers tell the truth) is to say something useful from the vantage point of younger women, I will try to draw out how splitting women into two types still functions within the

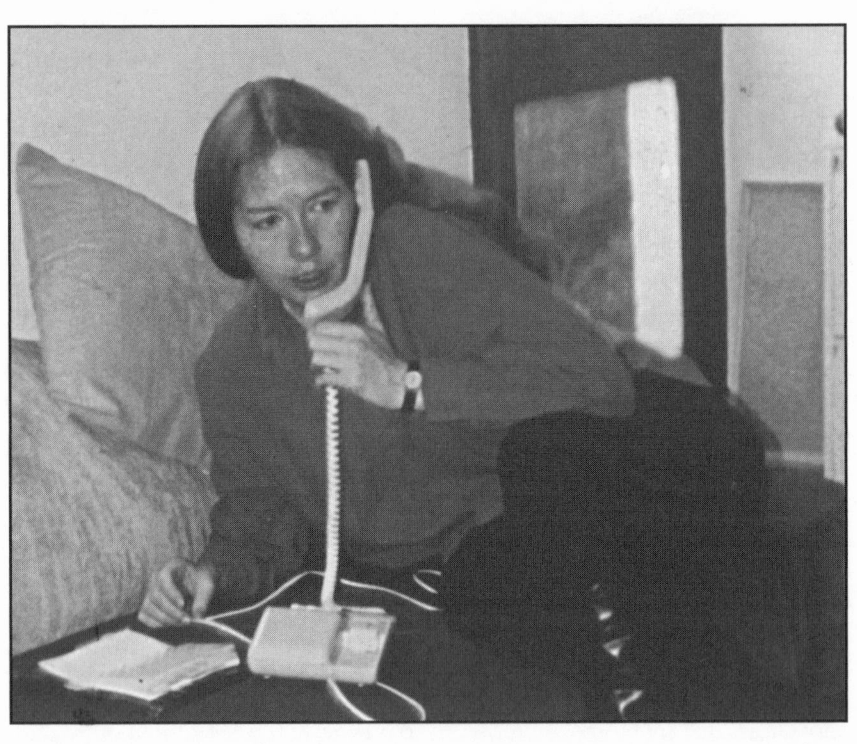

academy, by concentrating on my graduate and part-time teaching experience at Cambridge in the United Kingdom (1982–1993). This is not to suggest that Cambridge is the only place that my gender has affected my scholarly life; my prior experience in Sydney (from leaving school in 1969 to leaving Australia in 1980) also constitutes a gender story, as does my experience in the United States (1994–present). But these experiences have been or are of a different order, and they are more positive socially (if not intellectually). I found after the fact that (for some) I had carried a whorish (negative, seductive) projection in Cambridge. It had, and still has, effects. But before coming to this account, I want to frame the issues with a few notes on my background when I went up to Cambridge and King's.

After the radical past typical of the intellectuals of my generation in Australia (anti-Vietnam, antidraft, early women's movement, inner-city housing, women's refuges, and undergraduate life interrupted by politics and time out working for causes), I commenced an analysis with R. A. (Ron) Brooks in 1977 at age twenty-five in an attempt to work out why feminine masochism undercut creativity. I was teaching part-time, dabbling with a master's degree, and working for more causes. I had no serious thoughts of a career, but I did have serious thoughts on many books I wanted to write, which I imagined would vaguely take care of whatever needs I might have. I hoped (if I could find funding) to return to Cambridge, which I had visited the year before, to write a dissertation. If possible (I had no idea how I would pay for this), I also wanted to train as an analyst or train to analyze children.

Some months into the analysis with Ron Brooks, I had what has been termed a "conversion." Without at all wishing to aspire to the grand company that these names evoke, similar episodes have been described by Pascal and Jung (among others). Jung, whom I refer to with difficulty because of a personal dislike for his disloyalty to Freud, described his experience as "an upheaval from the unconscious, with enough material to last a lifetime." For Pascal, the experience was specifically Christian, as it was in my case. The essence of such an experience (I researched them at the time) is inspiration with ideas or a central idea from which other ideas grow logically. One is aware that the ideas are a gift. This is (or should be) humbling.

My work after that was based on those ideas and their elaboration. I was a thoroughly lapsed Catholic who had never made a decision to leave the Church, but I had distanced myself as feminism, Freud, and Marx took over as my explanatory tools for understanding the world. What was puzzling to my friends was that after the conversion, my theoretical vocabulary did not vary: my inspiration expressed itself in Freudian and deeply feminist terms; in some respects, it merely accelerated the question-and-answer process that Freud and feminism had begun. (The most influential books of my undergraduate life had been Juliet Mitchell's *Psychoanalysis and Feminism*, and Alice Clark's *Working Life of Women in the Seventeeth Century*, of which more soon.)

As conversion experiences were not de rigueur among Marxist–feminists in Sydney in 1978, I shortly thereafter lost various friends (except for Linda Barnett, whose love kept me writing) and was not reappointed to my untenured university post. Had I had my career wits about me, I might have opted for a Ph.D. in an "irrelevant" (to use one of the Borgian adjectives of the period) theology department. But I stayed doggedly in social and political philosophy; my place was with the feminists, with the Marxists, with the disputatious, and with the readers of critical books (I was unaware then, however, that these types were already taking over theology departments). In fact, thoughts of a Ph.D. of any sort faded. As I elaborated the central idea (concerning how the subject/object distinction distorted logic as well as perception) from that conversion, it seemed to me most urgent that the political implications of this theory were put into practice. The subject/object distinction has political implications? Certainly, as many feminist theorists have established. One can follow those implications via the circuitous route of the mind–body split (which I did). But perhaps the most useful thing I have done is to argue that the subject/object distinction distorts the labor theory of value by pitting "labor as the living subject" against "dead nature and technology as object," when nature also lives. Making a long theory short, this failure to take account of the manner in which natural energies other than labor power also live and produce surplus value (in that the value they add is greater than their cost of reproduction) led Marx to neglect how the tendency of the rate of profit to fall was offset by surplus value extracted from nature. Taking account of the fact that the real distinction Marxism had to offer was that between the living and the dead led to the conclusion that socialism had to give way to regionalism and localism in production. Pivotal in this turnaround, from the global to the local, were and are women as mothers. Alice Clarke in 1919 compiled an impressive registry of how women, as mothers, had greater economic and therefore greater political and social power before the onslaught of capitalism, precisely because home and workplace were not as a rule divorced.

By the time I worked this argument out (late 1979), various events were propelling me to leave Australia, including the experience of being stalked, which was to continue for another eighteen months; this was on the cusp of the period where allegations of being raped, harassed, or stalked were still taken as evidence of feminine pathology. I was unable to continue analysis, as I had no money by that point, but I could work. Enough so that in July of 1980, I was at Copenhagen for the UN conference on women. There I met a U.S. congresswoman, Barbara Mikulski, who also became convinced that the ideas I was writing should be put into practice. This marked a turning point, so before I leave this period, I add that while I was largely friendless at this time, I was not without support. Three members of my family were in Europe: my cousin Sally, who outwitted the stalker when he turned up there; my uncle

Keith, who had a residence not even the most determined stalker could penetrate; and my aunt Flora.

In November 1980, I joined Barbara in Baltimore, and shortly (and disastrously) afterward, I joined her staff. Together we devised legislation supporting the establishment of neighborhood business co-ops for working mothers and limited international trade among them. It was women as mothers who were affected by the separation of home and workplace that accompanied capitalism. Our policy was to reverse this separation. Barbara's staff were disaffected because I was very arrogant and because Barbara very much preferred my policies. They went to the press after a mass resignation and said that Barbara had fallen under the influence of an un-American Svengali type who was using her sexual wiles to steer Barbara away from Baltimorian virtue and toward "man-hating Marxis[m]." No consideration was given to the possibility that Barbara (one of the few intellectuals, then as now, in the U.S. legislature) was convinced by the power of ideas, rather than my twenty-nine-year-old charms, for the influence I had was, of course, sexualized and witchified in line with the stereotype mentioned at the outset. The reality, however, was different. After I joined her staff, the closest Barbara and I came together was to go to a Carmelite retreat on one occasion and share a tent on the El Salvador border on another (with six other women, two of them nuns, and background gunfire preventing sleep for us novices all night).

A word at this point on my sexuality, as my critics seem to find it so fascinating. After the conversion, which occurred shortly after turning twenty-six, I ceased sexual activity but concentrated on analysis and meditation. This decision was not a conscious one. I saw and currently see nothing wrong with other-regarding sex. It just so happened that I no longer had sexual desire of the kind I had known, and I was writing with an ease that made the process even better than sex. Of course, Freud describes this scenario as sublimation, which is in fact what I was doing, although I did not think much about it. But whatever grace enabled me to do so I lost toward the end of that year (1981) in Washington.

I have to be careful in describing what happened then, for words that are ill chosen could lead the reader to the wrong conclusion. The fact was that I was violently assaulted by two strangers. I think this experience, like that of being stalked, was at one level bad luck. However, given that confessing to a conversion experience (at least in the critical theoretical circles in which I move) already raises issues of self-delusion in the mind of the average agnostic reader, I need to stress it because one of the best-known syndromes documented by psychiatric enquiry is that characterized jointly by narcissism (or megalomania) on the one hand, and paranoia on the other. The assault and so forth was real. The conversion was internal. In fact I should probably say more about the psychology of conversion as such, for this is very different from the bolt from the blue the word conjures up, and the manic persecutions of the "born again." Janet Soskice (in a personal communication) described hers in terms of the serene sense of the immediate and absolute presence of love. I add that this sense of love (which is also the sense of loving intelligence) really is tangible; it is felt in the senses as well as the mind. The multideterminations of the sense and knowledge of presence is why those who have conversions describe them as the absence of doubt. In my case I became gentler and more tolerant, and more psychologically healthy to all intents and purposes, which is why my analyst passes over the conversion as an aberration to this day and thus recommended me for training in spite of having confessed to it. But the point was that if one acknowledges a conversion, the most common psychological interpretation is that one is having a narcissistic experience in which one is chosen. The conviction concerning the reality of the experience is understood as psychotic. It matters not that the other marks of psychosis are absent or that some events are indubitably real. In fact I did not feel chosen—after the sense of loving intelligence wore off, I mainly felt worried about how to get it done.

I choose not to discuss the sexual aspect of this assault because I have found that to do so is to reinscribe it in some way—a frequent occurrence when physical and mental trauma are combined. Suffice it to say that the assault left me with minor brain damage, which is a troubling disability for a philosopher. I was fortunate in that the long-term damage only affected my ability to visualize (and paint) and to some extent my visual memory, but its most immediate effect was that I could not write. Literally, I could not form left-hand margins with my words. I would write in tight spirals because I had to see the words in order to recall the argument. There is a limit to how many words one can fit on a page. It was as if my ability to visualize had changed places with, or somehow been mushed together with, my ability to reason logically. I recall sitting for hours trying to will myself to write in straight lines. I remember being most reluctant to accept that there were some things will could not overcome. An event that takes place against one's will precisely damages the will as such (or can do). I was convinced, no matter what the brain experts said, that the failure of will was connected to feeling full of shame (a common response to sexual assault). From this experience, I learned about the transmission of affect. But I learn slowly in general, and it was twenty years before I was able to complete the book, whose outlines I had sketched at the end of the 1970s, before deciding that a political movement had priority over a book. Yet I completed the book with the extra dimension formed by my experience, without which I would have underestimated the tenacity of human shame and its relation to social pressure.

Despite writing against the mind–body split, despite knowing I had changed and that I had physical damage, I carried on as if will itself could undo the damage done to that will. Believing this, I wanted another analysis rather than meditation to improve concentration. The fact that I decided to do that analysis as part of a psychoanalytic training led me to the Tavistock in

London. I began writing poetry, set down with Guin Tufnell's flat (Guin, her brother Nick, and Vicky Hamilton were good psychoanalytic friends in that early recovery). But I was unable to begin writing anything substantial again until late 1985, and this was a master's thesis. In retrospect, this poor dissertation served as an awkward exercise to recover the craft I had lost. Three other things made that recovery possible: my supervisor, Professor A. F. (Foo) Davies of Melbourne University; the example of the women at the Tavistock in London (teachers such as Gianna Henry, and peers like Pip Northey); and learning that if I dictated a draft to an amanuensis at a word processor I could write—and therefore think—with something like the logic I had lost. I knew I could write again after managing to compose an infant observation report for Gianna Henry. I also knew that writing was what I must do. I was fortunate in securing a Ph.D. scholarship at that point, and that is the path I followed. By 1989, I was dictating at the speed of writing I had known hitherto, and now I write freely without the aid of an amanuensis (although I write better with than without). Whether this current situation is the result of the increased communication between brain hemispheres, which apparently happens in midlife, I know not. But my next book is on consciousness, and perhaps I will know then. Writing for me has always been an act of resolution, a means of making sense, and I find I change as I write.

Melbourne's Foo Davies was a greatly underestimated Freud scholar and member of that endangered species, good white men. He sought and found funds to send me to the Tavistock on the strength of some of the outlines I had written postconversion. Then he had to tolerate deep poverty of prose while I learned how to remember the threads of argument and (related) how to craft sentences. It turned out, after the master's was completed, that Foo had personal feelings, although he had given me no inkling of them through the five years it took me to learn to write again and complete the degree he supervised. To do so would have been against the code of his gentlemanly generation, which he practiced through psychoanalytic, feminist eyes.

Hence, when I went to King's in 1986, at nearly thirty-five, my most recent experience of male mentoring had been a healing one. While commuting to the Tavi, I had also lived with family near Cambridge from 1982. It was a time when Cambridge shared in my positive transference to people and things English (especially in the way that they keep their distance and do not yell). There, I began the business of rebuilding the persona deconstructed in analysis and then shattered by bad experience. I found friends with whom I could share most ideas for that glorious purpose: the sake of argument. Hence, I should stress to the reader that my experience in Cambridge was not simply or even mainly negative. I should also add that I was often ill-tempered and demanding, in a rather childish way, and that I really do not know how my new friends (in Melbourne, at the Tavistock, in Cambridge, in those early years) put up with me.

To go further into this period would take me into religious confessions that are not relevant to my career as a woman in philosophy, so I will only say that I had lost the affective dimension of faith (i.e., the belief in oneself and one's goodness before God), but the intellectual dimension remained, asking to be worked through and elaborated. It was a task I could not avoid—although I would have liked to avoid it. Neither need nor enjoyment in general are facilitated if one appears a little religious and therefore (potentially) crazy. In addition, I had made a wager with myself for the times I was without faith. If I could substantiate what I believed to have been inspired, then it was true. If not, I could relax back into the agnostic warmth of my peers.

This background is intended to indicate those things in me that would allow a projection of a negative stereotype to lock on. The sense of shame I carried was probably evident in all those unconscious giveaways by which others know us when we do not know ourselves, but its source was misattributed. I wonder, too, if there was not a temporal displacement, as if I were responding to or taking on an image more suited to my preconversion persona (that being the only other self I knew). Similarly, my "agenda" (as in, "she has her own agenda") was misperceived. That is to say, ambitious whores are meant to have agendas and plan, and I do. My agenda is to substantiate the inspiration that accompanied my conversion, but to do so in a way that establishes its viability or explanatory force (as in *Globalization and Its Terrors* and *Transmission of Affect*). I did not discuss this with any but the closest friends for pusillanimous reasons—fear of social ridicule and the like.

As I had sexual issues together with the wish to be loved (a variation, for Freud, of the need for social approval), I was also having love affairs—which in the next decade encompassed two and a half men, two of them younger than I, and only one of whom could have even the remotest claims to influence at the time. Despite this, my name was persistently linked romantically with that of my better-known referees, including Anthony Giddens. I have not slept with Tony. We fooled around a bit before my first conversion, but it came to nothing. Tony always acted with integrity. He was a good friend to me when my stalker turned up in London in 1980. He supported me when he thought I was right for the post, but he also opposed my admission to the Cambridge Ph.D. program, and a few years later, he voted against my appointment to the faculty. So much for (being seen to be) sleeping one's way to the top. Hannah Arendt (who reputedly had to endure the indignity of being termed "a Weimar flapper") said that any young woman who wants to be seen as a thinking being before all else and who would like not to be plagued by anxiety about career survival as she does so, must avoid being associated, however lightly, with a well-known man (whether she marries him or not). In the collective social fantasy, any success she has will be attributed to his intervention on her behalf. In reality, he will be petrified of intervening even when she warrants that intervention, in case it reflects on his social image.

The real story of how I came to be admitted to a coveted Ph.D. program in my midthirties, with scholarship, is very different. It was through the agency of women. While I was living in Cambridge, being analyzed, and studying at the Tavistock, Naomi Segal (who then taught French at Cambridge) and I founded a reading group so that local intellectual women, in and outside the university, could verse themselves in feminist, psychoanalytic theory. (I could talk; I just could not write.) Through this group, I came to know some remarkable women, beginning with Naomi herself. The formal obstacle to my admission to the Ph.D. program was lack of a supervisor willing to supervise a dissertation on psychoanalysis and feminism in social and political theory. So we had to find a supervisor. Cambridge would not insult one of its members by declaring him or her as unsuitable supervisor, so Naomi (in French) asked Lisa Jardine (in English) for help. Lisa (who found psychoanalysis absurd in its phallocentrism) was then a primary port of refuge for embattled women graduates. She agreed to supervise nominally until we could sort out a permanent supervisor. We never did; Lisa saw the dissertation through to the end, and her genuine and practical feminism was worth a thousand fights about Freud. (I also learned something, not much, but something about late-Renaissance literature.)

Throughout the decade I was there, I experienced two Cambridges, which I will call Cambridge A and Cambridge B. In the realm of Cambridge A, the social Cambridge, I offended women and men I did not know or know past a superficial social interaction. In the realm of Cambridge B, the thinking Cambridge, I had a group of (principally) women interlocutors whom I came to know well. These women were intellectually exceptional and exceptionally generous. Sitting in Marilyn Strathern's kitchen (in 1984) discussing the subject/object distinction remains in my memory, but such things were then daily events. These Cambridge women appeared desirous of nothing more than discussing ideas as such, irrespective of whether those ideas had social currency. This experience was such a relief after the political correctness of Cambridge that I clung like a limpet to their intellects and only detached when forced to do so by those I had offended in the social.

From the social Cambridge A, I received an image that is familiar to many straight women. The image is that of a ruthless, manipulative woman streaking her way over dead or at least exhausted (male) bodies to the top, having hitherto slept with such of those men who could assist her rapid rise. At least it was a change (although not much of a change) from the devouring lesbian of Baltimore. As I said, I was in general ignorant of bearing a negative stereotype when I was in Cambridge. However, I did note (one could not avoid noting) that other women were spoken of as whores or sluts, and this surprised me, as I thought civilized people had stopped doing so under the influence of feminism, however diffused (and it was very diffused in Cambridge). I thought that one thing feminism had brought home even to its critics was a critique of the double standard and the split stereotypes (good wives and whores) that support it. Yet here I was, sitting down to lunch with people who told me how that Italian woman bonked a lot and how that Australian did, too. For, it was not English women who were spoken of in this way, only unmarried women who were also white colonials or southern Europeans. If the rate of bonking was reckoned in terms of changing partners, the unmarried English were on a par with the Italians. But the English were let off the charge of using men to advance their careers. The Italians and Australians were not. Why?

It irritates my English friends (in Cambridge B) when I refer to white colonialism because they do not practice it and therefore do not see it. But it does exist. It is present in the introductions before a college dinner in Cambridge A: "This is Teresa Brennan. She's from Australia, but she's really quite intelligent." Now no one would dare say it if I were from Ghana. (They would have just thought it.) But it is said to me and other white colonials, and we thus have to decide every time whether we are going to respond with compressed lips (a very important social signal among the English), with the standard self-deprecating silly grin, or let loose and ruin dinner for the innocent bystanders. English social signals warrant at least one dissertation in anthropology. While I may seem facetious in referring to them here, I am convinced that they are means for negotiating the transmission of affect, residues of a code of courtesy that once made sense as a generous means for nullifying the negative emotions. They work on the assumption that the real level of communication is at the affective level, and that words are mere means for negotiating those affects, but they are not subordinate to them. Nonethless, one has to deal with "She's from Australia, but . . ." unless Gillian Beer or someone like her does what she once did for me, which was to take the butter most wittily to task. The reason why Australians and Italians and Canadians were viewed as sleeping their way to the top, while English women were allowed to sleep untrammeled, has been stated elegantly by Norma Fuller. The person who belongs somewhere else but is there at a college dinner is a *parvenu*. A parvenu is someone who has crossed class or racial or colonial or gender boundaries not only once, but twice. They are women first, and on top of that, they are from Australia, or Italy, or somewhere other.

But as I said, it never occurred to me that I was one of the women spoken of "that way." I was far too occupied deciding if I was going to try (again) to sleep with anyone—or try (again) to regain the joy of sublimation I had lost. However, I learned that I had also been granted membership in the sleeping-their-way-to-the-top brigade toward the end of my time in England, after I had been unsuccessful in repeated applications for posts, thereby demonstrating the height of the top to which I had ostensibly slept. By 1990, I had applied for every conceivable post in Cambridge without success, except on one occasion. On this occasion (for a joint post at Pembroke and Girton), the philosopher and historian of philosophy Susan James was on the committee. The story I was told by others was that Sue (whose courtesy is almost Chinese) simply referred the discussion back—whenever it wandered—to the published work of the candidates. Because of Sue, and a committee prepared in the end to make an academic decision rather than a social one, I was offered the post. I declined it because I had been offered a full professorship in Europe, and the glamour of the appointment beguiled me. But I was unprepared for the aggression of academic politics outside Cambridge (I have an absurdly thin skin in this respect) and had to leave. In fairness, I should add that when you are stabbed in the back in Cambridge, it is generally done over good food with excellent wine so that by the time the knife goes in, one hardly feels it. I prefer this to people's rushing me in the corridor with drawn swords.

After leaving Australia, cantering around the States, settling in Cambridge, and then attempting Europe, a somewhat agoraphobic attitude to moving again might have kept me working in Cambridge part-time had not Drucilla Cornell picked me up and set me on my feet in New York. Drucilla invited me to debate Heidegger and mysticism with herself and Derrida, and as a result, Judith Friedlander, then dean of the New School (where the debate took place) offered me a visiting appointment.

The New School. Home of the Frankfurt School in exile and Arendt. That was where I belonged. But one day, I was told that a leading behaviorist psychologist N—— (ex-Cambridge, then at the New School) had visited the dean to express his alarm at the prospect of my receiving tenure there. Teresa, he is reported to have said, is a dangerous, ruthless woman who sleeps her way to the top. She also "exaggerates" (which, when given verbal quotation marks, is British for anything from "is balmy" to "not to be taken seriously"), but it is not something she can help. A bit of a pathology really.

When I asked for details of my pathology, the most I could learn was that I was meant to have had some kind of religious episode in Sydney (this was interpreted as a breakdown) and that I was meant to be a fantasist, who could not write or think but fooled people with jargon and superstitious dabblings with Tarot cards. (This one verges on calling me a witch outright.) Anyone who reads my work on femininity knows that I am, if anything, an antifantasist, believing that nothing interferes with release of creativity more than daydreaming—all educational circumstances being equal. My religious arguments are, I hope, distinctive in the contemporary context because they "privilege reason and logic in a manner surprising for a feminist." (Rachel Bowlby wrote something like this: Rachel, much love, and apologies if the words are inexact.) But it is only slowly that I have learned that there is not much point in seeking to know who started claiming imaginary conquests (making it easy for others to do the same) in which I feature as witch whore rather than as logical virgin (and if I denied it, that was a further instance of my making things up). For the real point is that a fantasy of women as whores or virgins structures perception in ways that mean the details—meaning the facts—are inconvenient.

Facts rarely match stereotypes. Hence not knowing, or barely knowing, the woman who is stereotyped is, I think, a condition of circulating gossip about her which denies her capacity for feeling (the ruthless exploitation of wounded men). I am told that a source of stories about me is a woman I have not met, a Charlotte someone. On receipt of the original version of this sketch, N—— (whom I have met once) denied that he had ever gone to the dean. Perhaps in N——'s case my informant made it up, or exaggerated details. My difficulty with episodes such as this (especially in the United States) is the verisimilitude with which people lie. On the one hand, when they deny in rage, I think they cannot possibly be lying. On the other hand, in his first public lecture at the New School, N—— described me as a "paranormal fundamentalist," which does not suggest he had been misinformed. But the social is a slippery thing, and those who purvey it seem ignorant often of doing so. I suppose no one is going to say, "Well, yes, I did go to the dean. I was a snob, and I had heard you were not the right type. However, I am now a recovered snob, who has begun to think about the psychology of types." But one can hope.

Those who are most prone to possession by the social are those who are most concerned about their social images. My impression is that the social is transmitted through affects, especially the affect of righteous indignation, and this affect is easily aroused whenever social image is negatively affected.

It is very easy to confuse the feeling of righteous indignation with doing the right thing. But as the expression, "the righteous gentiles" suggests, one is more likely to be righteous in fact when the force of social pressure is against one. Otherwise, the feeling (or strictly, the affect of righteous indignation) fuels the projection of "bad" onto another (woman, ideology, country), which it seeks to shame. Writ large, we see it in the response to terrorism, where many luxuriate in the righteous other-damning affects associated with standing for freedom. Righteous anger fuels the projection of "the bad" in the act called judgment, and it is the means by which the image of badness is made to stick. My rapists felt righteous anger as they brought a woman (who in their fantasy was already a whore) to their version of justice. That they did so outside the law and with violence serves to differentiate their actions from those who merely stereotype in social gossip, but this distinction should not blind us to the continuity of the affect between the acts of calumny and those of rape. Social pressure also goes outside the law when it denies due process; it leads others to act on secondhand righteous judgements without knowing both sides of the story or giving whoever is damned by those judgments the right to confront their accusers.

The following story indicates how critical it is that those who circulate the gossip stereotyping a woman as a ruthless sexual predator do not know her (although they may claim to know her to make themselves interesting). It also shows how common and repetitive such fantasies are. Once on a plane trip, a young Indian was given racist treatment by the steward. Of course, I offered to be a witness for the incident. I do not recall his name, so I hope he will excuse me for telling this story, as I have been unable to contact him in advance to show him this typescript before publication (as has been done with others). He was a sociologist who told me about a woman at a well-known university of whom everyone had to be wary. I had never heard of this woman (an anthropologist named Barbara?), and one or two questions led me to realize my fellow passenger barely knew her (if he knew her at all). Yet he was not to be deterred from telling me everything (allegedly) from intimate details of her personal life to how she had (yes, you guessed it) slept her way to the top, ended friendships, formed new ones, and generally held others enthrall against their better judgment (against their will?). But "to give the devil his due . . . you have to acknowledge that she did set up that anthropology center." This is the sentence I remember most clearly. I made a lay diagnosis of an acute case of unconscious envy. I use "unconscious envy" in Melanie Klein's definition, which finds envy manifested in destructive criticism. It sees the grapes, but before it can admire, it stops itself: it decides that the grapes are not beautiful; the grapes are sour.

Barbara, whoever and wherever you are, you are not alone. Your story helped me forget my concerns with "who started this?" It drew me back to the fact that what started this was a fantasy. Some people, especially (but not only) those of the male persuasion, see the world through this fantasy. An individual—whomever of the many men I have offended—is responsible if he invokes this fantasy, by adjusting the facts just a little to fit it. Yet even that adjustment, as I suggested, may not be a matter of a conscious lie, but rather, it may be of the way in which perception is filtered in terms of fantasies manifest as stereotypes. In turn, the thing that fuels those perceptions is social pressure, together with the denial of creativity in the feminine. Mothers are meant to serve, not think. Whores are women who do not serve men without demanding payment. If a woman, especially a woman men find attractive, is evidently not serving a man in her life, it is assumed that she must be serving herself. The fact that she might be serving something other than a man or herself—such as philosophy or even the literal love of Sofia—is not considered. Now, putting my own experience, Barbara's image, and other incidents together, I am more and more convinced that the envy of creativity lies at base of the image projected onto me and other women like me. The hypothetical support of supposedly credulous men explains whatever recognition the woman may have in terms that deny her labor as well as her intellectual capacity. This is where envy kicks in. On Klein's definition, "envy" denies creativity by attributing its results to anything other than creative labor. It denies it not only by calumny, but by making the envied creativity invisible. Where possible, that labor will be appropriated and attributed to men (as in the classic cautionary tale for young women scientists, about how Crick and Watson were awarded a Nobel prize, which they shared with Maurice Wilkins, but not Rosalind Franklin, who first identified the structure of DNA. At thirty-one, Rosalind Franklin was appointed to a research post working with John Randall at King's College in Cambridge. In *The Double Helix*, James Watson depicts Franklin as an underling of Maurice Wilkins, when in fact Wilkins and Franklin were peers in the Randall laboratory. But it was Franklin alone whom Randall had given the task of elucidating DNA's structure, and it was Franklin alone who first identified its famous double helix. Randall presented Franklin's data and her unpublished conclusions at a routine seminar. Then her work was made available—without Randall's knowledge—to her competitors at Cambridge. Watson and Crick then used her data without acknowledgment (mothers are meant to give for nothing) in building the final account of DNA's structure in 1953.

People can choose to believe things at odds with the evidence and still call themselves adherents of reason or rationalism, as opposed to advocates of superstition. If they have read my work and admired it, if they then hear that it is all jargon rather than the "logical unraveling" they took it to be, and if they are then told I cannot write when before they rather thought I could, what do they do? Some hold to their judgements, some scurry back on side with social pressure.

Where I draw the line is between those who think on the basis of the evidence and those who ignore or misrepresent the evidence so that it will conform with what they have been told to think. In doing so, they tell little and constant lies to themselves, and they then find themselves telling those lies to others. They do so because they do not believe in themselves or in the goodness of their judgments, and they wish their judgments to coincide with those that are socially validated. But because they do so, they know that somewhere, there is someone who is a bit free with the truth and who sacrifices it if it is to their social advantage. There is someone who is not rational but superstitious, someone who throws free reason to the winds and serves instead the dark forces of social pressure. This person is not loyal to their friends if acknowledging them in this or that social situation would be a minus rather than a plus. Who is this person? Who lies and manipulates and rises socially on the bodies of their friends? Goodness knows, they tell themselves, it is not really I. It is some other, someone else, someone beyond the social pale. And whomever that person is, they are not part of *us*.

To be afflicted with the social (I argue in the book I am working on now) is the same thing as being afflicted with a dishonest and therefore slower mind. But for our immediate purposes, it is enough to show that Cambridge A is slowed down by the social, which is why the best conversations about ideas now happen in Cambridge B. It is also why the neglect of feminism (misunderstood as some kind of ambitious philosophy unfair to men) undermines the genuine concern with the advancement of women in Cambridge. I do not want to say that life has been easy since leaving, but it has at least been free of the cruder sexual stereotypes that accompany patriarchy, and because of this, I have been employed, and even tenured, in the United States.

The rest of my career illustrates something that was clear at Cambridge, which is that the good things I have had in this profession have come through the hands of women, with two exceptions. A. F. Davies was one; Malcolm Bowie (who also read my work and offered me a post on the strength of it before we met) is the other. But in general, it has been women, from Philipa Rothfield and Kwok Wei Leng, who stayed up all night to help me get that initial master's degree in on time; from Sue James in the interviewing room to Drucilla Cornell; from my cousin Sally Brennan, who believed I was not mad when I most needed someone else to believe that, to Harvard's Alice Jardine, who protected me in all my initial and subsequent professional encounters in the United States; and most recent, Linda Alcoff, who asked me to write this piece because she was getting tired of doing battle for my social image with those who do not know me: it is these and other women who have secured security for me in this profession.

In 1998, twelve years after I commenced my Ph.D., I read an article in the Cambridge alumni magazine (*CAM*) on the failure of women to advance in the university, despite manifest concern for their advancement. I wrote a letter to the editor about the use of feminist theory in the context of concern for the advancement of women.

Dear Editor,

I was surprised to learn that Kate Pretty believes that Cambridge 'no longer offers any barriers to anybody who wants to rise up the system [and that the] barriers are within the individuals themselves' (CAM, *Easter term 1998, p. 21). Similarly, I was troubled by Mistress Pretty's idea that most women lack 'single-mindedness' and the capacity for 'sheer unadulterated hard work'* (CAM, *p. 20). While I agree with her that 'many women simply are not prepared to put work above everything else', and choose a baby rather than a book* (CAM, *pp. 20–21), more needs to be said about why this is so.*

The observation that the formal obstacles have been removed, but lo! the women are not getting on with it, reminds me of the oft-quoted remark made after suffrage did not yield more women parliamentarians. 'The cage door is open, but still the canary does not fly'. The remark was quoted often in the early days (1969–1975) of the second women's movement by writers advocating the idea that 'the personal is the political'.

The personal was key for many reasons, but the one at issue here is the way that informal sanctions were and are used against women who do not conform. These sanctions are based on a woman's personal life rather than her capability or attainment. In my experience, if a woman does put her work before all else, including (and this is critical) her emotional life, she will be fortunate to be described as single-minded. She is more likely to be called 'ambitious'. Ambition, used in relation to a woman, often means not caring for others, meaning, really, a man and family. Women are meant to care, to put care for others above single-mindedness about their own work. A man does not have to choose between 'a baby or a book'.

The essence of the procedure here may be summed up in the term, the double-standard. Briefly put, this meant that a good woman, by definition, was not single-minded. She was standing behind a good man. If she was not demonstrably involved in the caring female functions, and if there was nothing physically wrong with her in the sense that she was 'attractive', she was suspect. It was assumed that she must be of the scarlet ilk, as somewhere, somehow, the patronage of men had to be there. If it was not, then it was just possible that a man (and thence by implication men) were not of major relevance in her life. For some reason this thought is intolerable.

It will of course be said that all this is passé. But I for one do not know of any leading woman intellectual who is unattached (or even if she is) who is not said to have 'used men'. This idea may have its comforts to those who have not done as much or as well (male or female). And the notion that men are 'used' also serves to reinforce the belief that they are relevant.

But still, I should apologize for covering territory that would be familiar to any moderately informed student of the late twentieth century. The only reason for doing so is my concern that this double-standard does still operate at Cambridge, and that its stereotypes are active in the minds of many, even if they are unrecognised. Stereotypes, for example, in which an accomplished woman is presented as an ambitious, voracious devourer of vulnerable men. Or as pathological. Or sometimes, by those for whom logical consistency is not a requirement, both batty and successfully ambitious.

The manner in which this double-standard functions as a sanction is evident in the way that other women fear identification with the wrong category. Often it is women who will be first to criticize those who have, by repute, 'used men' to 'get to the top'. Such criticism, based on the most second-hand of reports, has an iconic function. It says: 'I am not like this, fear me not. I am a good woman, not a scarlet one'. There are complicating factors here of course: to my knowledge, the women who fill this iconic function in Cambridge are southern European or in some way other (not British). Whatever the case, students are not immune to the message. They hear the way that 'ambitious women' are referred to in their colleges.

As Cambridge is concerned for its female students, an active opposition to this double-standard, of the idea that you are not the right sort of woman if you really put your work first, is surely a priority. Awareness of the way 'ambitious' women are spoken of may even be why 'women take fewer risk' (CAM, *p. 20). Combating this may do more good than teaching male dons to be gentle or sensitive in supervisions, a procedure which does after all assume less intellectual robustness on the part of women. Unless of course 'being sensitive' is a synonym for damming up that vast reservoir of polite aggression that is still directed, via everything from hearsay to unemployment, towards a woman whose mind is on her work.*

Teresa Brennan
(King's 1986)

That was the letter I wrote. This is the letter published in the alumni magazine (*CAM*, Michaelmas 1998):

A woman who puts her work before all else, including her emotional life, will be lucky [I wrote "fortunate"—evidently the editor gauges this word too difficult for the average reader of *CAM*] *to be described as single-minded. She's more likely to be called 'ambitious', which means not caring for others—above all a man and family. Women are meant to care: to put care for others before their own work. So a good woman, by definition, is not single-minded; she is standing behind a good man.*

My concern is that this stereotype is still prevalent in Cambridge: that many think accomplished women are ambitious, voracious devourers of vulnerable men—or alternatively, pathological or plain batty. Since the university is concerned for its students, it should actively oppose the idea that you are not the right sort of woman if you put your work first.

Teresa Brennan
(King's 1986)

I do not think that there was anything other than a concern for editorial brevity in the editing of the letter. Yet one does not have to be a literary critic to figure out that all references to the double standard have been censored. Feminist theorists have analyzed how splitting women into two types perpetuates discrimination, but this analysis has been rendered incoherent. One might say that, of course, a truly sexist establishment wishes to ignore feminism, and that unvarnished sexism of this type is inevitable in a ruling-class institution, but it is not. The situation is both similar and different at Oxford, as I learned during a recent sabbatical. But Oxford's somewhat more evolved feminist and feminine consciousness has been pushed into being through open arguments and the strong feminist theory and women's studies programs, which Cambridge still lacks. Because of Alice Jardine, Juliet Schor, Susan Suleiman, and other strong feminists, even Harvard established a women's studies program. Not gender studies, but women's studies. As Jardine argued, the difference between the two is that women's studies, as such, signifies an ongoing commitment to redressing the imbalance that exists in reality among the genders.

Any feminism confronts stereotypes and how they work through social pressure to reinforce discrimination. But I do not want to say, and I do not believe, that it is only men who are steeped in the social in this way. Blaming the victim (from the lazy poor to the women who ask for it) requires a stereotype with an entrenched hold on the imagination, of the poor themselves, and of women. We are complicit with the othering intrinsic to stereotyping women as virgins or whores, and good or bad mothers, when we dissociate ourselves from the wrong sort of woman and do not temper the inevitable jealousies of our degraded profession with an awareness of their gender bias. I wish I had objected when I heard Italians and fellow Australians spoken of as women sleeping around but ever upward to get ahead. I wish I had made a good old-fashioned feminist fuss, and it is no good telling myself that it was the 1980s and that I wanted a quiet life. Because when a fuss is made, this generation, whose men also yearn for approval with a yearning that tempers their good judgement, learns. They learn that perceptions they took for truths are in fact projections of fantasy. They believe in the fantasy because they cannot see to read, and they believe in hearsay because they cannot hear when asked to think.

I learn, too. From these experiences I learned that the just woman or man is one who acts on his or her private convictions in public, and that being justified is a state in which one consistently withstands social pressure when its interests do not coincide with what one believes to be right. I learned that every mistake I made is the consequence of giving into social pressure. I also learned that a real friend is a person whose attitude to one in public is the same as their attitude in private (within reasonable limits).

The force of social pressure is what fuels the circulation of familiar sexist stereotypes, and it varies according to the honesty of those present in any gathering. In the United Kingdom, I found the splitting of women into good and bad types figured in the classic terms of virtuous women and whores. In the United States, and among feminists, the same split is figured in terms of good mothers who serve, and wicked stepmothers who frustrate their children's careers and more or less eat their young. When I was harrassable, I attracted more projections of the former order; now I sometimes attract the latter, but I attract it only from those who do not read and think and from those who give salacious hearsay special privilege. Nor, as should be abundantly clear to the readers of this collection, am I alone in attracting such projections (although I do seem to be good at it). Lacan said that without the splitting of women into two types, good women (who marry and are serving mothers) and whores (who do not marry and are not serving mothers), the patriarchal social order will collapse. If he is right, it behooves every thinking woman and every just man to refuse that split. But to do so is not easy. The rationale for Lacan's conviction lies buried, partly, in Freud's great observation: "Where they love, they cannot desire, and where they desire, they cannot love." Why does desiring and respecting a woman at the same time imperil the patriarchal social order? The short answer is that a man who desires and respects comes uncomfortably close to the feminine position. He comes close to the position that he associates with powerlessness. The fact that his power is maintained by setting women against one another—by dividing them into two categories—is not something he need consider while women themselves perpetuate the categories, fearing that if they challenge them—in what they say or what they write or how they live—they, too, will fall off the respectable edge of feminism into the abyss where identity is not mediated by the social, but a matter between oneself and God.

3

Finding My Voice: Reminiscence of an Outlaw

Claudia Card

Often, when I am asked how I came to be who I am, the subject is my lesbianism. In 1990, however, I was asked to write about how I came to be a philosopher. What emerged was the story of my learning to integrate being a philosopher–teacher at a state university with being a lesbian–feminist, and, finally, to write in a voice that I could call my own.

Becoming a philosopher can be a lifelong process. This is a story of how I learned to speak with my own voice as a lesbian–feminist philosopher with a certain set of histories. It is not about how I first chose philosophy—a tale, in my case, of adoration for teacher and texts—but about how I have been able to continue with philosophy. I have had to find and help maintain communities of women to keep growing philosophically. The result has been intellectual development in directions I could not have foreseen.

In the early 1970s, I was in my early thirties. Soon after I was tenured at the University of Wisconsin, I developed a writing block, which was to last several years. I had taught and written through reflection on the written word, but not otherwise out of my life experience. During the late 1960s and early 1970s, I taught an undergraduate course, "Crime and Punishment," which was popular and seemed highly successful. My students then were being arrested for crimes ranging from window trashing on State Street to ripping the flag from the top of Bascom Hall in the heart of the liberal arts campus. A small Stop & Shop grocery near campus was nicknamed "Stop & Rob." When a large Kroger-chain grocery near campus went up in flames, a local counterculture news sheet referred to the bystanders exchanging their "Kroger smiles." Some had graver encounters with crime. A woman student in my honors introductory philosophy class was found murdered in front of Sterling Hall in the spring of 1968, apparently interrupted on an early-morning campus walk.[1] Two years later, a male

student, also in my honors introductory class, made the FBI's Ten Most Wanted list in connection with the 1970 bombing of Sterling Hall—home of the Army Math Research Center—which killed physicist Robert Fassnacht.[2]

After writing an undergraduate thesis *and* a graduate dissertation on theories of punishment, and then publishing an article defending mercy and another defending retributive justice in legal punishment, I had begun to wonder what it meant that I was mesmerized by such topics. I had never been inside a prison. I had never witnessed an execution. I had never even attended a criminal trial. Nor was I close to anyone who, so far as I knew, had. None of that deterred me. I had read many books and articles that taught me to identify with the perspectives of lawmakers who may never have had such experience either. A combination of public events and events in my personal life soon led me to see that I did not yet have, or know, my own philosophical voice. I did not yet know how to speak or write from my position in the universe of space and time but only from my position in a universe of books.

My parents divorced after thirty-two years of marriage and four children, and then died within eight months of each other in the early 1970s—first my mother, during the year that I was tenured. I began thinking in new ways about who I was, perhaps deciding who I wanted to be.

During the late 1960s and early 1970s, two things were sending young white middle-class U.S. citizens to prison, many of them students, for whom the experience proved a field trip to study the criminal justice system. They were mostly men who might otherwise have arrived at my point in their careers with no more firsthand knowledge of that system than I had. The two things for which they went to prison were marijuana and war resistance. Soon, my "Crime and Punishment" class was populated by students who had an intimate acquaintance with the workings of criminal justice and related institutions. This fact became evident when several voluntarily presented their papers to the class. I had asked the students to begin with the point of view of someone who might be accused of a crime or someone who might be victimized by a crime and to search for a solution acceptable from both points of view. A devoted student of John Rawls, I sought wisdom in the area of justice through the hypothetical reasonings of ideal legislators who would identify with both sorts of possibilities. At the time, I assumed that since in reality anyone might either be accused of a crime or be victimized by one, everyone should be motivated to empathize with both perspectives.

The students' presentations were autobiographical, highly personal, and very moving. They were not typical philosophy textbook examples. Men spoke first. One had been sentenced to a drug rehabilitation center. Another was confined in a navy brig for the crime of smoking grass. One was assigned guard duty at the Camp Pendleton prison. Others were arrested in war-related protest demonstrations. One was assigned alternative service as a conscientious objector. Encouraged by their classmates' frankness, women spoke up who might otherwise have kept silent. One, institutionalized at the age of thirteen by her father for being out of his control, had recently been released *in her midthirties* thanks to the efforts of a woman worker in the institution. Another, found "not guilty by reasons of insanity" of the murder of her husband, had done time in an institution for persons so declared. The last speaker was a young man convicted of child abuse who had done time in both a regular penitentiary and an institution for the criminally insane, as required by the law of his state. Not claiming innocence and yet outraged at how he was judged and treated, he appeared little more than a child himself. The class, visibly disturbed, tried to engage him in thinking how to protect children from abuse.

The students tried, with amazing goodwill, to take up the perspectives of the assigned journal articles and textbooks. They tried to see crime and punishment through the eyes of the designers of penal institutions and to make that vision fit with those of people liable to suffer from such institutions. In doing so, they struggled with perspectives that did not fit their own well. I was struck by discrepancies between the results of their attempts and the assignment as I had originally envisaged it. Most of the philosophical literature that I had assigned seemed inadequate to get at the points of view of either those likely to be accused or those likely to be victimized (often, of course, the same people), much less to reconcile those points of view.[3] Instead, the literature offered the visions of men writing from the safety of not having to think much about *either* potentiality, overseers involved in neither the workings of penal systems nor the activities calling their machinery into action. Who *was* most liable to being accused of crimes or to being victimized by crimes? Not (conventional, economically privileged, mostly over forty, white male) legislators—but rather the very young, the homeless, the poor, people of color (in this part of the world), women attempting to protect themselves or their children against battery and sexual abuse, rebellious women who refused the "protection" of men.

Take myself, for example—a young lesbian (thereby, an outlaw) from the rural village of Pardeeville (Wisconsin) catapulted by scholarships from village high school to state university and then by fellowships to Ivy League graduate school. I was living in one of the highest crime areas of the city in which I taught, without a car, with no more than the simple hard-won financial security of a monthly paycheck, in an abusive, closeted lesbian relationship. I knew firsthand the fear of life outside the classroom and the library. Surely it was an escape. I began to suspect that much of philosophy as I had learned it served interests opposed to my own. A grant that I received to study the history of U.S. penitentiaries and other prisons helped me confirm that suspicion in detail. How could I avoid abandoning or compromising my truths while making "satisfactory progress" as a philosopher? I had reached a point in my life where I seemed unable to do either.

As my mother was dying, the university was deciding the fate of my employment, and I was stumbling through the crises of my first explicitly lesbian relationships, I also embarked on the first of two stages of feminist awareness. Both stages required intellectual interaction with women. I knew almost no other faculty women. There was no women's studies at Wisconsin (or most places) prior to 1975. A closeted lifestyle precluded my developing close friendships, even with the other nontenured woman in my department. My first intellectual community of women was a Consciousness-Raising (CR) group that met weekly there for years, consisting of mostly graduate students in philosophy and in computer science. I was the only faculty member. The nonhierarchical structures, narrative style, and respect for emotion that characterized CR groups were things that many of us later tried to bring into our classrooms: we experimented with "rotating chair" encouraged autobiographical writing in philosophy papers, took responsibility for exploring anger and fear in the classroom.[4]

A second stage of feminist awareness began when I connected with the Midwest Society of Women in Philosophy (SWIP), two years after the CR group disintegrated. The SWIP connection precipitated my exit from the abusive relationship. I was able then to "come out" in my work and at my workplace, thereby also becoming less vulnerable to future abuse. I became less blocked in my writing as I began integrating my "life" with my work. I began finding answers to the question of why I was spellbound for so many years by punishment and related topics. The CR group, SWIP, and, later, women's studies helped me heal and heard me into speech, enabling me to find and develop my voice as a philosopher who is, not incidentally, a semirural white Anglo woman, a woman-lover, and a survivor of domestic abuse—as well as the fortunate recipient of gifts enabling me to integrate these histories positively and put them to constructive use.

I found my (physical) speaking voice—a highly symbolic event—in delivering my "coming out" paper. On a warm day in May 1978, wearing a silver double axe (the *labrys*, a symbol of ancient Amazons) that swung on its chain as I leaned over my paper, I presented my "Feminist Ethical Theory: A Lesbian Perspective" to an overflow crowd of philosophers, women's studies faculty, students, and community dykes in a law school auditorium at the University of Minnesota. It was thanks to Kathy Addelson (then, Kathy Parsons) that I had the opportunity to do this. She was invited to present a paper on moral revolution, to which I had responded at an earlier conference, and she insisted, as a matter of feminist and anarchist principle (opposing hierarchies and heroes), that I be invited as well. The upshot was that each of us was invited to present a major paper and to comment on the other's major paper. Also, as a matter of feminist–anarchist principle, we occupied the stage jointly for both presentations. That level of support gave me new courage.

My paper was excessively long. After years of silence, there was too much that I wanted to say. But the audience was so attentive that you could almost hear them breathing. At the beginning, I announced, as usual, that anyone in the back who could not hear me should wave a paper or call out, and I would try to speak up. To my surprise, I began speaking from deep inside, without effort, in a large voice that I had not known was there. People later said they heard me in the hallways, even outside through open doors and windows. Anger fueled that voice, but also confidence (little inspires confidence like truth-speaking), despite some early anticipation of scorn ("what had that to do with *philosophy*?") from those I had been used to identifying as my audience. In fact, this audience received and discussed my presentation with more warmth and respect than I had observed elsewhere in professional philosophy colloquia.

I am no longer preoccupied with the perspectives of ideal legislators, nor with punishment, nor with the criminal justice system. Yet, in my current work, I draw freely upon what I learned in those studies. While supported by the grant to study prisons, I made a point to learn all I could about women's prisons and women in prisons, accepting invitations to give public lectures on the topic (one broadcast by a local radio station). In studying theories of punishment and autobiographies of prisoners while I was myself living through an abusive relationship, I began making connections between the way battering works and the way punishing works.

The focus of my attention, however, has turned more to the good and evils of interpersonal relationships and to informal practices among those whose life situations are more like mine than like those of men who are apt to become legislators. My vision of philosophy has also evolved. I am no longer so absorbed in "eternal" or universal truths.[5] I seek wisdom not in relation to the abstraction of human life considered simply as human but in relation to lives fleshed out as gendered, as members of species, as having certain ethnic, economic, and religious backgrounds, even sexual orientations—things that vary, things that are *not* universal. A decade after affiliating with the women's studies program, I began teaching environmental ethics, and I affiliated with the university's Institute for Environmental Studies. I still teach from books, but with more varied authors. I have even begun to write books. But I also teach from my life, and my writing flows from that life, with an awareness of its finitude as well as from my reading (which is endless).

The audiences I now usually address in my work are no longer composed first of all of men who are oriented toward the men who have been conventionally selected as representative of humanity—many of whose works I nonetheless continue to read with profit. My primary audiences—those "in my head" as I write—now are composed of those who are in various ways more nearly my life-experience peers: mostly women, many lesbians, all with points of view shaped by surviving and resisting sexism, many shaped by surviving and resisting racism and other forms of oppression. They are my "juries" in the sense that their evaluations help keep me honest and growing. They enable me to write; they make me want to. I worry less how to make "satisfactory progress" as a philosopher. And I work productively, without fear of running out of things to say before time runs out in which I can say them.

NOTES

From: Claudia Card *Lesbian Choices* (New York: Columbia University Press, 1995), 11–17.

1. The murder of Christine Rothschild, to my knowledge, remains unsolved.

2. The student was David Fine. For a page-turning account of those times, see Tom Bates, *Rads: The 1970 Bombing of the Army Math Research Center at the University of Wisconsin and Its Aftermath* (New York: HarperCollins, 1992). According to Bates (p. 446), David Fine earned a law degree at the University of Oregon, was then denied admission to the Oregon Bar, and went to work as a paralegal with a Portland firm specializing in patent law.

3. I did, however, supplement the philosophy with autobiographical writings and letters, such as Claude Brown's *Manchild in the Promised Land* (New York: Macmillan, 1965) and George Jackson's *Soledad Brother: The Prison Letters of George Jackson* (New York: Coward-McCann, 1970).

4. For more on experimental pedagogy with roots in feminist activism, see Claudia Card, "The Feistiness of Feminism," *Feminism Ethics,* ed. Claudia Card (Lawrence: University Press of Kansas, 1991), 3–31.

5. See Claudia Card, "Removing Veils of Ignorance," *Journal of Social Philosophy* 22, no. 1 (spring 1991), 155–61.

4

Taking Oneself Seriously, But Not Too

Virginia Held

One of the thoughts that has helped me the most in trying to take myself seriously as a philosopher has been one I encountered in the early years of the women's movement that began in the late 1960s and early 1970s: consider whose opinion you really care about. Some women writers were then beginning to advise women readers to stop fawning on the established men of power in their lives and professions, and to pride themselves instead when other *women* thought well of them or their work. At the time, it was a novel thought. But I gradually came to care increasingly about the good opinion of other feminist philosophers, who occasionally were men but who were almost never well established. I cared more about them than I did about the invitations, which continued to be absent, into the circles of the philosophical elite at whatever level I was. I had been brought up with a kind of protestant reliance on individual conscience and disdain for popular opinion. Although such an upbringing helped me as a philosopher, approval was still needed not only for occupational survival or the effectiveness of one's efforts, but to think that one's work had merit—and approval had meant, of course, male approval, though I didn't think of it this way at the time.

Breaking the habit of looking for male approval and measuring one's own worth in terms of it was extraordinarily difficult for women of my generation, I suspect, since we grew up with such a dearth, as far as we knew, of women to admire. The few who had accomplished something seemed always to be portrayed as freakish: asexual, unfeminine, unattractive, or, at the very least, so totally atypical that aspiring to be like them seemed as irrational as expecting to win the lottery. Understanding how false this picture was developed only gradually. But develop it did, along with the goal of being admirable by criteria *we* determined to be acceptable, which came to be

feminist criteria. So the idea that has served me well is that the judgment that matters most is often not that of the philosophical establishment.

Another idea that has helped me is less specifically feminist, but it can often serve feminist purposes. It is that although I may not be very capable or competent at all, I may be not very much *less* capable or competent than others who occupy the positions they are already in. Many of the professors of philosophy I encountered were not extremely talented, well prepared, brilliant, or entertaining. It was therefore comforting to think that for a position comparable to theirs, I *should* only need to be *as* capable, rather than greatly more so. Whether I would actually get a job or not were I only as capable as they were was, of course, another question, but at least I didn't feel undeserving of a job.

When I was recently slated to give the presidential address to the eastern division of the American Philosophical Association (APA), I felt, despite having been elected to this position, extraordinarily anxious about and inadequate for the task. It appalls me now to remember that in a difficult moment before this talk, I was actually comforted by the thought of George W. Bush. I told myself that if someone so obviously inadequate to the task of being president of the United States could actually occupy that office, I ought to be able to at least give a talk to the APA. The thought that women of all races, classes, and ethnicities, as well as men of groups previously excluded, will not do less well the jobs that privileged men have all along been doing not very well should strengthen the ambition of many, including the young philosophers struggling to find jobs and recognition in the profession.

It was also a surprise to me that I was so very anxious about giving the talk to the APA since none of the earlier sources of major worry (like needing a job or tenure) had any relevance and since I had by then given literally hundreds of talks. Perhaps if I had picked a topic that was more routine for me, I would have been more confident. But when I chose the topic, I thought I had plenty of time to figure out how to make some points I had long wanted to make. And as the date approached the degree to which I was locked into that topic and those points increased. I suspect that even if I had decided on a different topic, the occasion would still have elicited the kind of trepidation I had felt in earlier years because of the feeling that I was—more than at any previous stage—an interloper into the next rank of the favored. Even though I might not especially value the opinions of many of these favored, the feelings of the past of being dependent on them for continued life as a philosopher reappeared. I was reminded of how, decades after I had received a Ph.D. and was safely tenured, I could still not enter, even just to listen to a paper, the seminar room in the department at Columbia from which I got my degree without being made extremely uncomfortable by the recollection of being a graduate student at the mercy of the philosophical fathers, where the philosophical sons all seemed so articulate and where I seemed so tongue-tied. It has taken me years and years of practice, mostly in teaching, to be able to speak more or less freely in public.

In the days before my APA talk, the well wishes and encouragement I received from feminist friends were enormously sustaining. In the earlier trials, however, I had had no such friends. None of us understood what a feminist support system was. If young women today think they no longer need any such thing, and if they are right, it is enormous progress indeed.

In the 2001 movie *Legally Blonde*, a ditsy-looking and airhead-behaving Valley girl decides to get serious. In a top Eastern law school, she works hard, gets good grades, and hopes the professor she is working with thinks well of her work. As her confidence grows, the professor makes a pass at her, and she is demolished. On the verge of giving it all up and going back to California, a hitherto decidedly unsupportive older woman professor, who by chance hears about the situation, dissuades her.

I recognized the devastation, having experienced it especially in the interval of work before teaching philosophy and writing my dissertation. I had no one to advise me to persist since it did not occur to me to talk to anyone about this sort of thing. I thought I was not naïve, my youthful explorations having been sexual as well as intellectual. But I was unprepared for the undermining it brought about to be thrown, from the plateau of aspiring employee or student, into the category of sexual prey. I was highly naïve about that. I did not understand it as the generalized attack on women's advancement that it often was, and, of course, there was then not even talk of the harassment that later led to rules advising superiors to be on guard. I gradually suspected what was going on when men felt their intellectual and occupational superiority challenged. What confirmed my impressions was the sharing of experiences so characteristic of the women's movement that was beginning to develop just as I was winding up my degree in 1968. But for years, I lacked the self-esteem that might have been strengthened by having an established philosopher think well of my work. Even when some actually seemed to approve of it, such philosophers were always male, and I could always suspect their motives.

I was saved once from giving up by the fortuitous timing of the acceptance of a short article by a philosophy journal. None of the editors had ever met me, so I knew their motives could not be mixed. I was saved another time in graduate school by reading a short article by Kate Millet on the sexism of some of the great writers who have been widely admired and whom I admired as well. It was one of the very first feminist analyses I had ever encountered, and I cannot overemphasize the way bits and pieces of writing I encountered, usually by chance, served as flotation devices when I felt I was sinking. I had never found time for de Beauvoir's long book. I had heard it dismissed as humorless, and I did not know enough to wonder why on earth this extraordinary account of the long history of women's subordination—

w[illegible]ourse, I later read—should be expected to be funny. But at the ti[illegible]ed them most, in lieu of feminist friends that didn't yet exist, there w[illegible]sional and very lonely feminist words that could be read; quite possibly, I would not have been able to continue in philosophy without them. I did have one woman friend in philosophy before any of us became feminists: Judith Jarvis Thomson. We had been undergraduate classmates at Barnard, but she had gone on in philosophy much more directly than I had. By the time I returned to it, she was so far ahead of me and so successful that I could not see my own chances as in any way comparable. But she did advise me on what to expect if I returned and on how to proceed, and that advice was indeed helpful.

Several years after getting my degree, tenure gave me the feeling that I was out of danger of drowning. I suppose that the climate has changed sufficiently that young women today may wonder if the approval of their work by their women professors is unduly colored by sentiments of solidarity and is hence less than impartial. But they can always compare such judgments with those of their professors who are men. We could not make such comparisons when I was in graduate school because there were no professors who were women in the programs most women my age attended. I suspect that despite distinctly improved conditions, young women philosophers today still have some trouble taking themselves seriously.

We certainly do not want to turn into the arrogant, aggressive, disdainful, and self-important male philosophers we have all too often encountered, who are models of those who take themselves too seriously. They provide the extreme from which to stay away as we seek the right balance of self-confidence and modesty. We may have few historical models to show us where the right balance is for women philosophers, but that gives us just one more issue to explore along with all the others.

I have not yet said anything here about being a mother along with being an anxious young woman seeking a place in philosophy. Having two small children while pursuing a Ph.D. obviously had its additional stresses, to say the least. I thought the images of mother and of philosopher in the minds of my professors were so completely inconsistent that I never spoke of my children or brought them to the campus I lived near. I didn't need to lie because conversations were in any case minimal. But it took me many years to outgrow, myself, the internalized distortion acquired in that prefeminist age, that one could only be a philosopher when one forgot that one was a mother. Gradually bringing these two selves together subsequently has been an important source of theorizing for me, as well as being a vital contributor to personal well-being.

My husband got his first adjunct teaching job, which was his first job since starting graduate school, as I was in the hospital having our first child. I continued working part-time and went back to graduate school around the time we had our second child, and then I started teaching part-time. I received no financial aid whatsoever during the entire time I was in graduate school. It had been pointed out to me without embarrassment that my employment prospects would be very limited since most philosophy departments did not hire women. I could surmise that for my graduate school department to take a chance on using its limited funds to support someone who was not only a woman but also a mother was clearly an unpromising investment.

My children were a source of strength, however as well as one of difficulty. It was while I was pregnant with a first child and still working for a magazine that I found the courage to write my first article. I thought that if I fail miserably as a writer, at least I'll still be a mother. When I was in graduate school and crying after failing an exam for which I had found no time to study, my son, then about two, asked why I was crying. When I told him of my failure, he climbed on my lap and said, "But I love you just as much." And I could try again.

Our lack of money in those years complicated the stresses. However, if we had not needed the money I made, I probably could not have justified, even to myself and certainly not to my husband and wider family, working or studying for the sake of future work. Those were years when mothers were expected to devote themselves entirely to their children. If they worked when they did not need to, they were seen as unbearably selfish and as taking themselves much too seriously. So in that way, I was fortunate to have a good excuse to work, however little time it left for sleep or unhurried play with my children. Later, as our marriage gradually fell apart and as I needed even more than before to provide for my children—knowing that although I could tolerate poverty for myself, I could not impose it on them—I was impelled to strive harder and get more done faster than I ever could have without the desperate urgency. For many years, I was on the verge of crying much of the time.

One aspect of taking oneself seriously is taking the issues one cares about seriously. I loved philosophy from the time I took my first philosophy course in college and decided almost immediately to make it my major. But I abandoned it after one year of graduate work in Europe with a Fulbright grant. I did so partly because my husband was a graduate student and partly because one of us had to work. Another reason, however, was that it seemed to me impossible to deal within philosophy with the issues of war, deprivation, injustice, and inhumanity that I had come by then to care about the most. Ethics was then a largely sterile kind of metaethics, and anything else of a normative kind was thought "unphilosophical." But after some years of working at a magazine and discovering the way independent thought was discouraged outside the university, I then returned to philosophy. By the time I got my degree, the field was beginning to be dramatically transformed, and it was possible to deal with actual moral problems in philosophically acceptable ways. I was deeply involved in the New York City area in trying to make this happen, through meetings and gatherings to hear papers. The primary occasion for this shift was, I think, the Vietnam War, which led many philosophers to protest U.S. policy and to become actively engaged in dealing philosophically with the moral problems of civil disobedience, resistance, and political change. The civil rights movement had paved the way, and the publication of John Rawls' *A Theory of Justice* in 1971 gave an enormous boost to the entire, then moribund field of political philosophy. I had gone back to graduate school knowing that I wanted to work on the concept of the public interest since it seemed to me so essential and neglected. The public interest became the topic of my dissertation.

Other trends besides the civil rights movement and the war in Vietnam contributed to the change in philosophy that enabled more and more philosophers to move beyond a restricted metaethics and to combine normative theory with the consideration of actual problems. During the time I was in graduate school, an established British philosopher, one of the few women in the field, was scheduled to give a talk at my department. She had scrawled the title of her paper on a card, and the men of the department were handing it around trying to decipher her writing. They said it looked like "abortion" but it couldn't be that, they thought, because that was not a philosophical topic. It turned out that her paper was indeed on abortion, and soon thereafter, one paper after another handled this subject in ways that were obviously philosophical. Then, a variety of problems in what came to be called "medical ethics" gained attention. Before long, combined with such issues as capital punishment, war, famine, and a few others, "applied ethics" became an area in which students could take courses and in which philosophers could find employment.

Many of us argued, and still do, that "applied ethics" was not the right name to call this inquiry into actual moral problems, since it was not a matter of accepting a worked out moral theory and simply "applying" it to various problems. The theories should, rather, be put to the test of experience with actual problems; thus, they should be modified as needed and improved through the process. In turn, theory itself should be developed on the basis of practice in dealing with the moral problems of various contexts. If a philosopher is asked, for instance, to serve on a committee at a hospital to deal with the moral dilemmas that arise in providing medical care, the philosopher had better become knowledgeable about and understanding of the practice of medicine and how hospitals work. Otherwise, the philosophical perspective may be of limited worth. Something comparable holds for anyone developing moral theory in any domain, so "applied ethics" may be a misleading term. But whatever it is called, that philosophy now acknowledges its legitimacy is significant progress, though this progress is constantly in danger of erosion. Many philosophers, especially at institutions seeking most crassly to be elite, once again dismiss this kind of inquiry as philosophically marginal. But in view of the fact that applied ethics is an area of philosophy with better employment opportunities than most others, it is at least tolerated. And given how much the practice of moral inquiry in actual contexts can contribute to the improvement of moral theory, it can be expected that this tolerance and acceptance may sooner or later be appreciated.

The gradual strengthening of theory that can result from the combination of theory and practice is perhaps nowhere more apparent than in feminist theory. Feminist philosophy has by now become a more or less accepted part of the field of philosophy, with well-attended courses being offered and popular programs presented at the American Philosophical Association and other meetings. There is regular interaction with and learning from feminist activists and those dealing with actual problems around the globe, such as violence against women, denial of reproductive choice, discrimination in employment, and so forth. The improvements in theory resulting from contributions from the different perspectives of women of color and of postcolonial voices have also been enormous.

More women philosophers, whether they are interested in feminist philosophy or not, are gaining jobs and tenure. Philosophy as a gladiatorial contest is to some extent giving way to philosophy as a cooperative inquiry. Whether they participate in feminist inquiry or not, the greater presence of women in philosophy makes the field less inhospitable for other women and for feminist philosophy. That there is some residual disdain among males fearful of not maintaining dominance is hardly surprising and hardly a major obstacle. From where we are now, feminist philosophers can think of them largely as missing the boat, rather like white Southerners who cannot adjust to integration. The trashers of feminism, especially when they are women, may obtain conservative foundation support, press attention, and favorable reviews in journals that have not taken feminism seriously. But feminist inquiry and cultural change in a feminist direction, though maddeningly slow at times and seldom steady, continues. I believe that it is cultural change these days that leads the way to social and political change. Having been part of this development has certainly been gratifying.

5

Freethinking?

Alison M. Jaggar

To an alienated and rebellious schoolgirl in the late 1950s, philosophy meant freethinking. It represented a world in which people openly discussed topics that I pondered only in secret. As soon as I learned that this world existed, I wanted to enter it.

In 1960, I was nearing the end of a decade's imprisonment, as I saw it then, in an all-girls high school in Sheffield, an industrial city in Yorkshire in the north of England. Sheffield was a steel city famous for its cutlery (I believe that steel was invented in Sheffield), and my father worked in the steel industry. My parents' families had lived in the city for many generations; indeed, my father claimed to be able to trace his line back before the Norman conquest to a Saxon ancestor named Cudwulfus, reputedly so named because he had cut off a wolf's tail when out hunting. While I was growing up, however, my family lived in Dore, then a Derbyshire farming village surrounded by heather-covered moors, from where we commuted five miles into Sheffield for our schools and jobs. When I was a baby, lights were lit on the moors to mislead the German planes seeking to bomb Sheffield's munitions factories. Although the lights lured one bomb onto Dore, they did not prevent two extremely severe Sheffield blitzes. I am not old enough to remember the bombing, but in my earliest memories, Sheffield is a city riddled with bomb sites.

Sheffield's wartime heroism strengthened my parents' loyalty to the city, which blended with their loyalty to king (soon queen) and country and their allegiance to the established Church of England. (Like many in his generation, my father regarded the evacuation of the British army from Dunquerque by small boats sailing from ports around the coast of Britain as "a miracle in our time," God's direct response to prayers offered in churches all

over the country.) I was compelled to attend Sunday school, where I won prizes for attendance and for being able to recite each week's assigned biblical verse, and later I was forced to attend church, always wearing a hat and often wearing gloves. Compulsory religious training was also taken for granted at school: we had prayers and a hymn every morning, weekly lessons in scripture, and we beseeched the lord to behold us with his blessing as we assembled and departed at the beginning and end of each term. It is decades since I attended church regularly, but I still know by heart much of *The Book of Common Prayer* and *Hymns, Ancient and Modern*.

The version of Christianity that was imposed on me shaped my prephilosophical reflections. Alone in bed at night, I pondered the meaning of life and wondered if God and I were the only beings who really existed. I was especially fascinated by the question of how freedom of the will could be compatible with everything's having a cause; I struggled to formulate this question as I fell asleep. At church, I disagreed with the moral lessons drawn from several parables. However, such reflections were encouraged neither by the vicar of Dore (who prepared me for confirmation at age thirteen) nor by my teachers at school, all of whom made it clear that too much questioning on my part was impertinent. Instead, I was told to remember that, in the words of a popular hymn, God moved in a mysterious way his wonders to perform. When we read Milton's *Paradise Lost*, the English teacher banished me from class because I argued too stubbornly that, if God knew already that Adam and Eve were going to sin, they were hardly free not to do so. My mother reminded me, a little tongue in cheek, that speech was silver but silence was golden. She then quoted, "Be good, sweet maid, and let who will be clever."

Both admonitions were ironic. My mother was not one to remain silent, and she was determined that I should be clever. Unlike my father, she had a university degree, and she may have wanted me to have an alternative to the domestic role that she found so frustrating. My mother demanded that the cleverness she imputed to me should be confirmed by good school reports and eventually by winning admission to Oxford or Cambridge. She was enraged that my teachers consistently reported "Alison could do better." I thought my mother's expectations and my teachers' judgments were quite unjust: how did they know I could do better, since I never did? The demand to be clever but not too clever was only one of the confusing messages about gender that I received as I was growing up.

As I grew older, I found school and church increasingly boring and repressive, as well as very cold. (The joint on one of my little toes still does not work because of the chilblains I had every winter.) As a child, I escaped through fiction, though the public library in Totley, a couple of miles away, had only a small selection of books, very limited hours, and, when I was small, they only let children take out two books at a time. (Adults could have six books, and I begged my parents for part of their allowance.) As a teenager, I became alienated and hostile, constantly seeking corners of the school where I could hide to escape lessons, sports ("jolly hockey sticks" was an epithet for the athletic girls I affected to despise), and freezing outdoor lunch breaks.

The one activity about which I was enthusiastic was riding horses. After falling passionately in love with the beach ponies at Filey, a chilly seaside resort on the Yorkshire coast, I became a classic horse-mad English girl. My parents could not afford to buy me a pony, but from the time I was eight or nine until I was twelve years old, my one-hour riding-school lessons were the highlight of every week. As a teenager, I begged and borrowed horses wherever I could. I was active in the Pony Club, where I eventually became an instructor, and for a time, I even had some success riding competitively. It was through training unpromising horses rather than through schoolwork that I learned to work persistently for long-term goals. It was also by mixing with people who showed horses, foxhunted, and "evented" that I became aware of my own lower-middle-class status, which my Sheffield accent made evident as soon as I spoke.

Sheffield High School for Girls was founded in the late nineteenth century as an outgrowth of the women's suffrage movement. However, I had only the vaguest understanding of this tradition when I attended the school, and I was somewhat repelled by the severe portraits of the four founding mothers after whom our school houses were named. I certainly did not want to look like those worthy women when I grew up! At school in the 1950s, I received more mixed messages about gender. On the one hand, the school demanded high standards and encouraged university attendance, listing girls' most outstanding achievements on Honours Boards in the great hall. On the other hand, it was never clear to me just how we were supposed to use our education: I got the impression that university was a place where one would meet more interesting boys and perhaps marry one. A degree was presented as "something to fall back on," thereby qualifying us to support ourselves through school teaching if we were not fortunate enough to marry or if our husbands died—divorce was still rather scandalous. In addition to a range of academic subjects, including heavy doses of Latin, the school taught us domestic science (I broke several sewing machines), deportment (we had to walk with books on our heads), and ballroom dancing. Because I was tall, I always had to be the man, leading my partner through waltzes, foxtrots, and quicksteps.

Bertrand Russell introduced me to a thrilling world of ideas beyond the confining orthodoxies of school, church, and good manners. His *History of Western Philosophy* was available in the school library, and his account of the philosophical issues at stake in the seventeenth-century European wars of religion enlivened my hitherto lukewarm study of history and gave more focus to my own reflections. After devouring Russell's *Problems of Philoso-*

phy, I was inspired by his declaration that "the free intellect will see as God might see, without a *here* and *now*, without hopes and fears, without the trammels of customary beliefs and traditional prejudices." Philosophy seemed to offer a more satisfactory means of escaping conformity than my earlier methods of fiction and hiding, and I decided that I wanted to read philosophy at university rather than history. (I would also have considered anthropology, economics, and sociology if I had known that these disciplines existed.)

Oxford and Cambridge had very few places for women in the early 1960s, and such places had to be won through competitive examination. I did well in the exams, presumably helped by my reading of Russell, and I was interviewed at every college to which I applied. However, I failed miserably at the interviews. I was overawed by the gothic buildings, and I felt painfully provincial and lower middle class in comparison with most of the other candidates. They seemed to be sophisticated girls from prestigious boarding schools who spoke loudly in assured upper-class accents, sometimes mentioning connections with the "dons"—a word with which I was unfamiliar. (In general, "dons" are professors, but in particular, they are professors at Oxford and Cambridge.) I was acutely embarrassed by my Sheffield accent; by the stodgy tweed suit selected by my well-meaning mother; by my ignorance of contemporary arts, culture, and politics; and by the fact that my parents took the conservative *Daily Telegraph* rather than the liberal *Manchester Guardian*. I hardly spoke in the interviews and was rejected by every Oxbridge college I visited. So after leaving school, which I celebrated by burning my hated uniform hat on the netball court, and after working for some months in Belgium as an au pair, which taught me that I was not cut out for domestic life, I entered Bedford College of London University. My mission was to resolve the problem of free will versus determinism.

Bedford was a women's college, actually the first women's college in the country. Ironically, it was closed down in the 1980s by the first woman prime minister, who sold its buildings in Regent's Park. Like Sheffield High School, Bedford supported women's scholarship, but I perceived it as numbingly conventional, filled, I thought, by more of the good girls I simultaneously envied and scorned. The colors of its scarf were those of the women's suffrage movement—green (for liberty), purple (for loyalty), and white (for purity)—but I did not realize this symbolism until decades later. When I was a student at Bedford, I thought the dull colors of its scarf reflected what I regarded as the dullness of the place. However, because each philosophy course at Bedford required only one lecture per week, I was able to spend most of my time at the London School of Economics (LSE), which I found much livelier. It was full of radical ideas and men, including many Americans, white and black, who were easily distinguishable from British men by their height, their superior hygiene, and their dazzling white socks.

Although I enjoyed the political and social atmosphere at the LSE, that was not what drew me there initially. Instead, it was my undergraduate disappointment with philosophy. In high school, philosophers had appeared to me as daring challengers to conventional wisdom, and Russell indeed maintained that image. I once heard him speak at a Trafalgar Square rally of the Campaign for Nuclear Disarmament and was deeply moved by the tiny, frail old man with the mass of white hair. However, the other philosophers I encountered in London were less glamorous, and their writings were less stirring; even Russell's academic writings on reference and the ramified theory of types were less exciting than his popular books. The early sixties were the heyday of linguistic or conceptual analysis. Philosophers now took their mission to be that of deflating the bold claims made earlier in the century by such philosophers as Russell, the early Wittgenstein, and A. J. Ayer, whose iconoclastic *Language, Truth, and Logic* initially seemed to me a paradigm of philosophical reason defeating woolly-minded conventionality. I was reading philosophy to discover if people had free will, but the answers I found were disappointing. Antony Flew offered the paradigm case argument, according to which free will was manifest in the smiles of willing bridegrooms, and J. L. Austin fussed over the distinction between shooting a donkey by accident and shooting it by mistake. Metaphysics and epistemology were reduced to debates over the correct uses of language, and political philosophy had been pronounced dead. Historical philosophers were read as groping toward contemporary distinctions. I found some encouragement in Ernest Gellner's *Words and Things* and a volume of essays called *Clarity Is Not Enough*, but I could not see a philosophical alternative to the analysis of ordinary language. Desperate to learn something substantial, I discovered that the special topics paper in the philosophy degree examinations included an economics option, and so I took several helpful economics courses at LSE.

For three glorious years, I ran wild in London, but the days of reckoning arrived too soon in the form of nine final examinations on which one's whole degree depended. Shortly before the exams, one of my college friends discovered that she was pregnant. Since abortion was unavailable, she threw herself out of a third-floor window (in the United States, fourth), a drastic means of terminating her pregnancy that simultaneously broke her legs and back. After each day's exams, rather than studying for the following day, I would travel to visit Elizabeth in Hampstead Hospital.

My own panic at exam time was rather different. Uncertain about my ability to do well in philosophy, I hastily got engaged to marry an LSE student whom I had met two weeks previously. I must have viewed marriage as something to fall back on in case of academic failure. When it turned out that I had done well in my finals, the engagement ended as quickly as it had begun. However, I had absolutely no idea what to do next, since I had previously indulged in only a few vague fantasies about life after university. My real desire was to attend graduate school, despite my doubts about philosophy, but I had so little confidence in my philosophical ability that I never dared communicate my desire to anyone else. I therefore returned to my parents' home in Sheffield and, like so many young women with arts degrees, took a course in shorthand and typing, hoping to qualify for one of the so-called girl Friday jobs that dominated the sex-segregated employment advertisements. Today's young women can hardly envision the services expected under a job title that blatantly combined sexism, racism, and colonialism in a single popular expression that everyone understood. However, my sister remembers that the head of the secretarial course summed them up as follows: "A good secretary is an extension of her boss's personality." Since I was temperamentally unsuited to be an extension of anyone's personality, I also tried some substitute teaching in Sheffield elementary schools; however, because I lacked any training in education, each day was spent in crisis management.

The paucity of employment opportunities made graduate school seem even more desirable, but I had no idea how to set about entering it. I therefore arranged to go to tea with my old Bedford professor, Harold Acton, who by now had moved to the University of Edinburgh. My new boyfriend, a veterinary student named David, agreed to come and support my audacious plan of asking Professor Acton about the possibility of graduate work. David was different from other young men of my acquaintance partly because he liked horses—we had met at a horse-riding competition, where he represented Edinburgh University and I represented London University. However, David really won my heart by his scorn for my shorthand/typing course, which everyone else thought was such an excellent idea: another boyfriend of the time insisted on taking me to lunch with his sixteen-year-old secretary so that I could pick up some tips. Even with David's encouragement, it took all my nerve to raise the topic of graduate school with Professor Acton, but I was overwhelmed with relief when he did not find the idea outrageous and indeed suggested that I take the new master's of letters (M. Litt.) degree just instituted at the University of Edinburgh. My mother, always supportive of education, gave me three hundred pounds, and I began my graduate career.

I spent two years in Edinburgh, in the middle of which David and I were married in Dore Church. It seemed quite daring to substitute "cherish" for "obey" in the marriage service, but I was happy to take David's name, which to me symbolized not ownership by my husband but instead a new shared life of adult independence. Not everybody saw things my way, however. Most relatives other than my mother assumed that I would give up my graduate studies on marriage; one remarked caustically that I'd be better off taking courses in cooking than in philosophy. I remained in the M. Litt. program but was haunted by guilt over my "selfishness." David found a job working for a veterinary surgeon in Falkirk, a grim little town near Edinburgh, and it was taken for granted that, as his wife, I would function as an unpaid receptionist for the practice. His job ended when I was rude to a farmer who, despite his cow's having had milk fever all day, had waited until late Sunday evening to call for help. I supplemented our income by typing theses for male graduate students since, in the days before personal computers, men were not expected to be able to type. (In the late 1960s and early 1970s, more than one of my male students excused the lateness of his paper by explaining that his girlfriend had no time to type it.)

Most of the philosophy students and lecturers at the University of Edinburgh were male, and I was too intimidated to speak much in the seminars. However, the time in Edinburgh was a wonderful opportunity to explore my disquiet with philosophy and its methods. I found it very satisfying, even therapeutic, to write an M. Litt. thesis in which I challenged the prevailing idea that philosophy must be limited to exploring the "correct" uses of language. It included chapters criticizing Ryle's view of philosophy as logical cartography, and Wittgenstein's conception of philosophy as letting the fly out of the bottle. I rejected what was then called "the autonomy of philosophy," and I argued that supposedly descriptive metaphysics in fact was covertly prescriptive. Like most philosophers of the time, I focused exclusively on metaphysics, epistemology, and the philosophy of language, since moral and political philosophy were widely regarded as defunct. I saw no connection between the dominant approach in metaphysics and epistemology (which Wittgenstein called "leaving everything as it is") and the moral and political conservatism of the 1950s.

By the time I received my M. Litt. degree in 1967, this conservatism had cracked wide open, most spectacularly in the United States, which sent dramatic images of civil rights protests to British television screens. David and I were in no hurry to settle down to the highly gender-restrictive model of married life that was all we knew, and so, seeking adventure and the postponement of adult responsibilities, we set sail for the United States. Our destination was Buffalo, New York, where I had applied to do a Ph.D. at New York's expanding State University. I selected this institution partly because my confidence was still minimal; partly because State University of New York at Buffalo required me to request only two letters of recommendation; and partly because Buffalo was on the border with Canada (David had a license to practice veterinary medicine in Ontario). The voyage to the United States—on a ship carrying pot-smoking, guitar-toting students back from a summer spent hitching around Europe—provided a crash course in student culture and in especially the history and politics of the war in Vietnam, which preoccupied practically everybody. By the time we arrived in upstate New York, we thoroughly understood why several young men had sought sanctuary in a Buffalo church and why others were burning their draft cards.

SUNY, Buffalo, had a huge and very eclectic philosophy department, where I encountered philosophical traditions that I had barely known existed. They included phenomenology, pragmatism, Marxism, and existentialism—the last of which had been quickly dismissed by one of my British lecturers as based on a confusion about negation. I took courses in several of these approaches, but my indignation when their ideas could not be explained to me in "ordinary language" revealed that I was more deeply influenced than I realized by the British philosophy that I had thought I was challenging. I ended up writing another semitherapeutic metaphilosophical dissertation, this time focusing on problems of communication in philosophy. Under the direction of Newton Garver, I addressed the issues of translation and paraphrase, and I explored the ontological commitments of so-called ordinary language. (My first attempt to defend my prospectus was blocked by a male professor who was not on my committee but whose advances I had rejected.) My Ph.D. dissertation marked the end of my preoccupation with the nature and value of philosophy, largely because the political and intellectual ferment of the late 1960s pushed the discipline in new directions.

From the time of my arrival in 1967, the State University of New York at Buffalo was shaken by mounting protests about issues related to the expanding war in Indochina. They included protests about university defense contracts, campus military recruiting, ROTC, and, of course, the draft. They were also linked with broader critiques of U.S. society, especially the perceived authoritarianism and bureaucratization of the university. In the summer of 1969, Marilyn Myerson, another graduate student in philosophy, invited me to join a small group that was meeting to discuss women's liberation. I had not the slightest idea what this meant, but I found the meetings to be as revelatory as my early reading of Russell. Some of the women were in relationships with male campus activists and were very frustrated by their assigned role as what Lydia Sargent has called "housekeepers to the revolution," operating mimeograph and ditto machines, running errands, and providing sexual rewards for male heroes. One popular slogan of the time was "Chicks say yes to men who say no" (i.e., the draft resisters). I did not feel oppressed in my primary relationship—indeed, David found the new ideas as exciting as I did. However, the ideas of women's liberation explained many of my internal conflicts generated by the mixed messages I had received when I was younger. They offered a new perspective on my discomfort with my being engaged in a predominantly male discipline, with my lack of interest in domesticity, and with my height, which was a half-inch taller than the average British man, who at that time was reputed to be five feet eight inches. It was indeed liberating to consider that something was wrong with the prevailing norms of gender rather than something was wrong with me. I became an enthusiastic convert to the cause of women's liberation and immediately tried to convert my mother, who was rather insulted by my missionary zeal.

In academic year 1969–1970, the student protests became so intense that the SUNY, Buffalo, campus was closed for many weeks and occupied by the state police. During this time, the protesters offered so-called Free University classes covering a variety of topics. Among them was a course in women's liberation, offered by my women's group. The only relevant book with which we were acquainted was Friedrich Engels's *The Origin of the Family, Private Property, and the State*, but that was almost a hundred years old and hardly spoke to our current concerns. We therefore copied pamphlets and articles from the newsletters and magazines springing up all over, such as *Women: A Journal of Liberation*, published in Baltimore. A group of perhaps sixteen or eighteen women would meet one evening in someone's home to figure out a topic for that week's class, and the next day we would go out in pairs to "teach" material that we were just inventing. Marilyn Myerson and I worked together, and the ideas that we discussed in those classes became the basis for my later work in feminist philosophy.

Even though I had been educated in both a school and a college founded only seventy-five years earlier by British feminists, I did not learn the word "feminism" until 1970, during a job interview with an elderly male professor. The absence of this word from my youthful vocabulary shows how quickly and completely First Wave feminism had become, in Sheila Rowbotham's words, hidden from history. However, even if I had known the word "feminism," I'm not sure that I would have seen the women's liberation movement of the late 1960s as a continuation of what I then thought was merely a bourgeois struggle to secure the vote and property rights for married women. My generation—who came to be called Second Wave feminists—was inspired less by Wollstonecraft or Mill than by Marcuse, Memmi, and Fanon, and we took ourselves to be extending and deepening the ongoing struggles for what were then called Third World and Black liberation. Today, white feminists of the Second Wave are often portrayed as having been concerned exclusively with securing abortion rights and women's access to the professions. However, many of us aspired not to equality (with straight, white professional men) but instead to a radically new social order. We imagined that this would include the abolition of gender, race, and class, which in turn would require the disestablishment of the traditional nuclear family, referred to disparagingly as the "het nuke."

My first academic job was at Miami University of Ohio, most of whose philosophy faculty members were also young and fresh from seething graduate schools. African American philosopher Leonard Harris had just graduated from the master's program and left to pursue a Ph.D. at Cornell, after teaching a groundbreaking course in Black philosophy in the winter quarter of 1970. I was immediately given the assignment of teaching a course in the philosophy of women's rights, which I did in the winter quarter of 1971. I believe it was the first course in the United States on feminist philosophy. The class generated huge excitement in Oxford, Ohio. It was open to all, not just to matriculated students; it was held in the evening so that women with day jobs could be present; and it was usually attended by two or three hundred people, who saw it less as a philosophical exercise than as an opportunity for consciousness-raising. The wives of several of my colleagues even led discussion groups. In the absence of textbooks, they also helped carry to class huge piles of dittoed and mimeographed materials, some of which eventually made their way into the first edition of *Feminist Frameworks*, which Paula Struhl (now Rothenberg) and I published in 1978. Fortunately, two books had just become available to supplement that hoary staple, Engels' *Origin of the Family*. The new books were Robin Morgan's *Sisterhood Is Powerful* and Toni Cade's (now Cade Bambara) *Black Woman*, both of which addressed gender in the context of differences in race, class, sexuality, nationality, and age. I also devoted some class time to discussing issues of men and masculinity.

I spent two happy years at Miami University, where my philosophical, professional, and personal lives seemed for the first time to be in complete harmony. In the second year, David and I embarked on our first experiment in so-called communal living. Early in 1972, however, I found myself pregnant and so applied for a job at the University of Cincinnati, about forty miles away, where David was already working in the medical college. I was fortunate enough to get the job, though a colleague later informed me that I owed it less to my job talk on Quine's thesis of translational indeterminacy than to my miniskirt.

We stayed in Cincinnati for eighteen years, but I was never as comfortable there as I had been at Miami University, which was partly due to the fact that once again, in Bob Dylan's words, the times they were a-changing. As the 1980s succeeded the 1970s, students became less receptive to some of the material we read in my courses, especially my course on anarchism, though my introductory course on feminist philosophy never failed to draw a large crowd of people from the community as well as formal students. I was also unhappy because of my perception that not all my new colleagues regarded my work in feminism as "real philosophy," a charge to which I was hypersensitive because I still was not entirely convinced that I was indeed the sort of material from which real philosophers were made. Some Cincinnati colleagues were encouraging, but one was openly hostile and another thanked me for a reprint that I proudly gave him and told me that he would pass it on to his wife.

The hardest thing of all for me was dealing with one, soon two, and eventually three babies, all of whom revived my earlier feelings that it was selfish to pursue academic work. We lived in a house with several other people committed to child care, and Teresa Boykin even became a co-mother. Nevertheless and perhaps unreasonably, I always regarded myself as the parent of last resort, the one who could never refuse to look after the children when everyone else was too busy. I constantly felt that I was not spending enough time either with the children, preparing adequately for class, or committing enough energy to social activism. Writing philosophy seemed especially selfish, and I used to get up before dawn to do it. A more self-assured philosopher and mother would surely have balanced these competing responsibilities with less anguish than I did, but the demands of full-time academic work were (and still are) incompatible with prevailing expectations about motherhood. As the first tenure-line woman philosopher at the University of Cincinnati, I felt extremely apologetic about giving birth within a few days of starting my position, and rather than asking for release time, I rushed back and forth between home and campus to breast feed the baby. When the class was long, David would bring her in to be fed halfway though.

As I struggled to combine the various aspects of my life in practice, I was simultaneously seeking a theoretical integration of feminism with academic philosophy. At first I felt alone in this enterprise, but early in 1971, three women philosophers—Sandra Bartky, Ruth Barcan Marcus, and Fay Horton Sawyer—circulated flyers calling for a meeting in Chicago. I invested fifty dollars in a flight to what became the founding meeting of the Midwest Society for Women in Philosophy (SWIP), where I was delighted to encounter about twenty other philosophers who were also feminists. Some of those attending assumed that the main purpose of the organization would be to address discrimination against women in professional philosophy, but I was among those who were also interested in finding a philosophical language for discussing feminist topics. I distributed copies of my new syllabus, which were received with skepticism by some and with excitement by others, and the following year several more people began teaching philosophical courses on feminism. Sandra Bartky was especially enthusiastic, and for a time, I would mail her each week the materials I had just used. SWIP became a forum not only for discussing issues of equal access to professional philosophy, but it also became a place for exchanging syllabi and soon for trying out philosophical papers on feminist topics. Attending the biennial SWIP meetings, often accompanied by babies, became one of my highest priorities in the 1970s. As other members have written, SWIP provided indispensable support and intellectual community for women and feminist philosophers who frequently felt insecure and marginalized. Without SWIP, which soon developed sister chapters on the coasts, in Canada, and in the United Kingdom, feminist philosophy would never have emerged.

The encounter with feminism has transformed my original understanding of philosophy. As a teenager, I was captivated by Russell's account of philosophy as "abstract and universal knowledge into which the accidents of private history do not enter." I loved the idea that the philosopher's "free intellect" would enable him (and hopefully her) to transcend "an exclusive and personal point of view and a body whose sense-organs distort as much as they reveal." When I studied the Western canon, I found that Russell's aspiration to knowledge independent of time or place and that his adherence to the ideals of rationality, universality, impersonality, detachment, dispassion, neutrality, and transcendence were widely shared. In ethics, for instance, many Western philosophers postulated a "moral point of view" symbolized in metaphors such as a god's-eye view, the perspective of an ideal observer (or an archangel), an Archimedean point, or a view from nowhere. However, my experiences as a woman in an overwhelmingly male discipline have shown me that no philosopher is really a "free intellect" in the sense of being entirely liberated from the preoccupations and prejudices of his (or even her) particular time and place. I now have a more naturalistic understanding of philosophy as a culturally specific set of texts and practices produced by individuals inhabiting particular social locations and addressing concerns that are historically particular. In this view, philosophy is not an autonomous realm of pure reason; rather, it is continuous with the natural and social sciences, and with literature. Thus, it is best pursued through multidisciplinary approaches. For this reason, I find that my current twin appointments in philosophy and women's studies at the University of Colorado complement each other very well.

In 1886, Nietzsche wrote that "every great philosophy" is "the personal confession of its author and a kind of involuntary and unconscious memoir." I do not claim that my work is great philosophy, but it does reveal my personal preoccupations first with religious questions, then with the nature of philosophy, and finally with the ways in which the "masters" of philosophy have expressed the interests of their gender, race, class, and nation. However, Nietzsche viewed philosophy as more of an individual project than I do. My philosophical interests emerged in ways that were to some extent unique: my writing was more than personal confession because my concerns were not entirely idiosyncratic; instead, they were similar to those of many other philosophers of my generation. Thus, other feminists were ready to take up the project of investigating how the philosophical canon has been established—whose interests and authority have been promoted, inadvertently or otherwise, by its central concepts, ideals, and assumptions—and how it has discredited women, especially less-privileged women, and the culturally feminine. Of course, our specific social locations inevitably make it easier for us to perceive some things rather than others, and people are always readier to recognize others' privilege than their own. I am white, as readers have probably assumed from the first page of this essay, and my writing has been criticized for insufficient attention to race and ethnicity. I am still working to remedy this deficiency, especially by exploring and challenging the ways in which contemporary Western philosophy continues to reflect the neocolonial perspectives of those who dominate the present world order.

If philosophy is just like other cultural artifacts in reflecting the historically specific concerns and preconceptions of those who produce and consume it, must we abandon the idea that philosophers are freethinkers? Not necessarily. I no longer regard philosophy as the only, let alone the best, form of freethinking, but I still think it is—or can be—one form. However, rather than equating freethinking with transcendence of our own situations, I suggest that our thinking becomes freer as we increase our awareness of those situations and how they influence us. I am not saying that freedom is the knowledge of necessity; instead, I'm suggesting that increased awareness of what postmodernists call our own positionality enables us to question beliefs that we have hitherto taken for granted and that it opens up alternative ways of conceiving the world. Thus, as people enter philosophy from more diverse backgrounds, they challenge its dogmas and move it closer to the ideal of freethinking. My early attempts to combine feminism with philosophy were undertaken in the belief that philosophers' tools of logical analysis would help to clarify various feminist claims, but now I think that feminism probably has helped philosophy more than philosophy has helped feminism.

Feminist philosophy is still often misrepresented as concerned only with a narrow range of "women's" issues and maligned as insisting on "politically correct" dogmas. Increasingly, however, it is recognized as offering illuminating perspectives on most fields of philosophy. Participating in developing this approach to philosophy has been for me a deeply and highly gratifying life project. It has allayed my doubts about the importance of discipline; it has suggested topics of inquiry that continue to absorb me; it has supplied curriculum material that some students find transformative; and it has provided me with brilliant colleagues and lifelong friends. I consider myself fortunate to have entered philosophy just when the time was ripe for this development, and I also am fortunate to have come to the United States, which was far more open than Britain to varying approaches to philosophy—and where my accent suddenly became a cultural advantage rather than disadvantage. In addition, I consider myself extremely fortunate to have received the support from my parents, life partner, extended family, friends, colleagues, and children, who have all made it possible for me to participate in this work.

6

Etc.

Stephanie R. Lewis

My career path has a discontinuity in it. The first part, employment in academic philosophy, had a lot of twists and turns, and ultimately disappeared into a swamp. The second segment of the path, outside of philosophy, has been less convoluted. Running along next to both segments, but not really joining them, is a thread: my membership in, and activities in, the American Philosophical Association (APA).

My philosophical career began auspiciously, with my marriage to David Lewis in 1965. Apart from that, it was pretty rocky. For a start, I never did get a Ph.D. I was a graduate student in philosophy at UCLA for four years in the late 1960s, in the department in which David was an assistant professor.

After those four years, we spent a year at Oxford, where I was a semiofficial visiting student and trying to finish up what I thought of as my thesis. After that year, David and I moved to Princeton, where for ten years I led the life of an academic gypsy. I had seven separate one-year (or less) jobs, some part-time and some full-time, teaching philosophy at colleges and universities within a day's reach of home. It's not as if it was a choice between career and cohabitation: I don't suppose taking a temporary job further afield would have done anything more to advance my academic career than the jobs that I did get.

These were not the sort of jobs that further an academic career, though they did keep it afloat for ten years. I was, variously, an adjunct assistant professor, an instructor (half-time), a visiting lecturer, a visiting instructor, and an instructor. I taught beginning undergraduates, some precepts in middle-level philosophy courses, some junior seminars, and I supervised two or three senior theses for philosophy majors. I published a couple of papers and coauthored, with David, a couple of others, and I also gave talks in the United States, Australia, New Zealand, and Scandinavia.

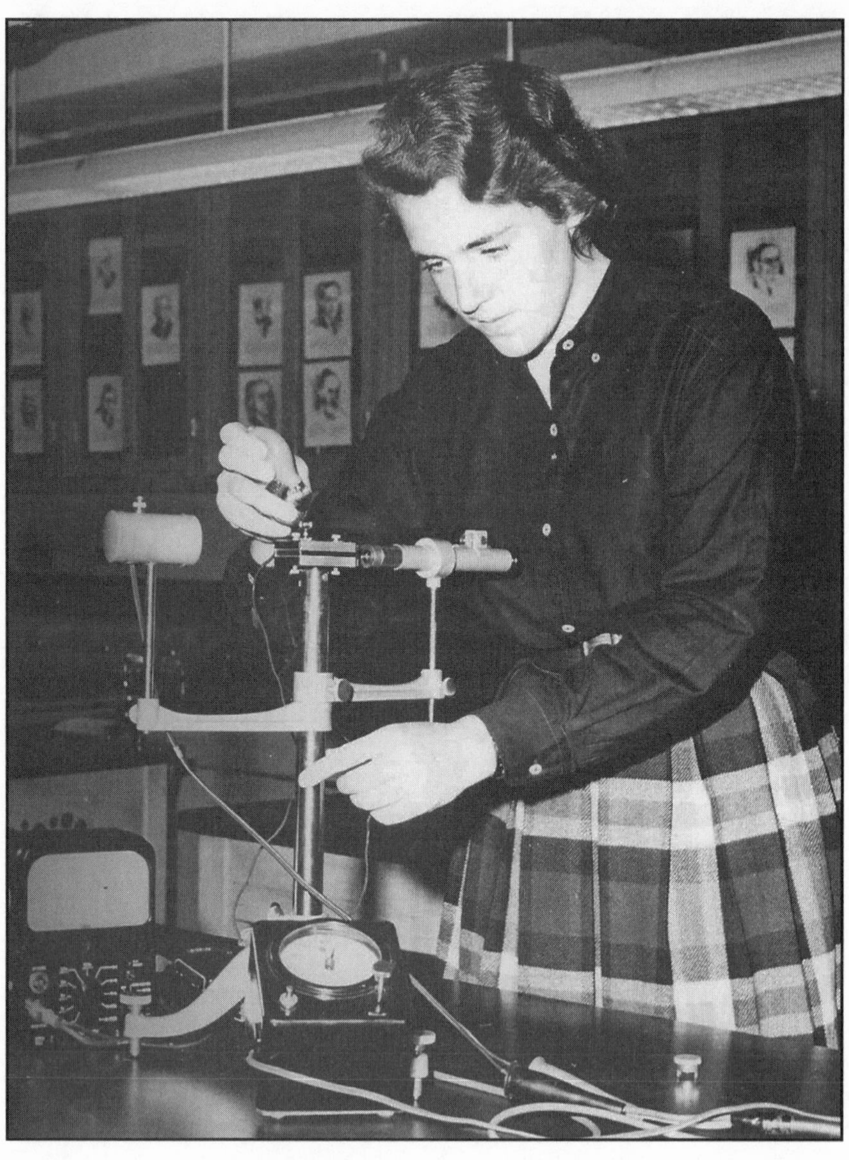

It wasn't really such a bad life. Unlike many itinerant laborers, I was nearly always treated like a member, if a short-term one, of the department I was working in. One year my employer even made retirement contributions. And I was always in touch with philosophers and their research in areas in which I was interested. I mention David because I firmly believe that my own path would not have been the same if I were on my own or with a nonphilosopher husband. Being married to a successful philosopher had three major effects on my own path. First, it kept me squarely in the middle of David's world. That was a world of philosophical conversations, colloquia, trips to philosophy conferences, and friendships with philosophers. Second, people who ought to have known better made some form of the following inference: from "David Lewis is a very smart person and a very good philosopher" to "Steffi Lewis is probably a smart person and might well be a good philosopher." And last, household income was secure and enough so that I didn't ever have to worry about where my next meal was coming from. This last is a very unusual luxury, and sets me apart from the great majority of people trying to make it in the underground academic economy. I cannot overstate its importance.

Part-time, short-term teaching jobs were, and still are, an iffy proposition. There never was assurance that something would turn up. For ten years, however, something usually did turn up, but it was impossible to rely on its continuing. Eventually, I woke up to the fact that without a Ph.D., I had absolutely no future as an academic. With a Ph.D., who knows? The 1970s were an especially bad time for beginning academics in the humanities. If I had thought that I had a fighting chance at a tenure-track appointment, the choice between cohabitation and career would then have become been a serious one. So I threw in the towel. I went to business school and got an MBA, and in 1982, I started off on my new career in municipal finance. Now, twenty years on, I still work in municipal finance. My job is to provide financial advisory service to cities, towns, school districts, and wastewater treatment agencies. (I used to say "municipal entities" until the La Trobe University philosopher Robert Fox reminded me that my ontology was a disgrace.)

The core of my job requires me to do cost and revenue projections for a wastewater treatment system, figure out the tax impact of constructing a new upper elementary school, structure bond issues, draft and review bond disclosure documents, calculate the rate impact of a new $7 million sewer outfall, things like that. I am also often asked to make presentations to municipal officials and members of the public, explaining their financing or capital project to them and trying to make it comprehensible, without either dumbing down technical material or evading questions that require detailed answers or lots of fiddly little details. Sometimes I even get combat missions . . . well, verbal combat. One project was to be part of a cadre that was trying to protect a perfectly well-run, harmless little municipal sewerage authority from dissolution at the instigation of the town's evil-hearted, moustache-twirling mayor. The mayor had an agenda, which I think had in part something to do with payback. We lost, and the authority is no more, but at least we slowed the other guys down and ran up the political stakes for the mayor.

Another assignment is not really combat, but is adversarial and politically charged. Between 1985 and 1988, a big but thinly populated township in New Jersey had a large development of condominiums and town houses constructed within its borders. Along with the housing, the developer provided infrastructure, including a collection system and treatment plant to handle the wastewater generated by the new development. Some other residential and commercial parts of the township connected to the wastewater treatment system; in addition, a couple of neighboring townships signed up to be customers of the new system, delivering wastewater and paying for the service at a bulk rate. Now, fifteen years later, the developer wants to get out of the wastewater business and has offered to sell the collection system and treatment plant to the township in which it is located. All fine so far. The trouble is the price. The developer started out by valuing the system at over $100 million and then knocked the price down to $70 million. At the request of the township, I looked at revenue and expense projections, then I set up a little spreadsheet model of the system's financial operations. Depending on which set of assumptions you think is most likely to reflect the real world, my version of the price came out between $7 million and $38 million. The developer came down to $57 million, and we revised our assumptions and came back with $23 million. (This is not an unreasonable price for a new system of similar size and technology.) Now it's their move. I had to present my results and the calculations and assumptions that went into them. This part has to be thorough and free of mistakes, and more important, it has to *appear* to be thorough and free of mistakes.

What I do is not philosophy. It has nothing to do with philosophy. I don't suppose that the philosophical literature has, until now, contained the phrases "force main" or "relief interceptor" or "inverted siphon," nor has it had an argument for the assertion that capital reserve and replacement funding needs to be taken into account in figuring out how much each user of a wastewater system will have to stump up every year.

But I do what I do in the manner of a philosopher. In the second of the two projects I just described, I had a couple of long conversations with an academic friend about strategy, tactics, and the substance of the presentation. The academic friend is an economist, not a philosopher, but it was the sort of conversation that academics have and upon which philosophy thrives. That conversation did make me think that if I'd had a thesis advisor like that, my life might well have turned out differently.

I joined the APA in 1968 as a student member, and I converted to full membership in 1971, when I got my first teaching job. I have regularly attended APA meetings, and I have served on several committees, including three terms as chair of the subcommittee on nonacademic careers. I am presently the treasurer, which carries with it membership on the board of officers and on the chair's council.

My membership in, and activities within, the APA are important parts of my life, and they have been for decades. Unlike nearly all other APA members, I don't have to worry about my own career advancement in philosophy; I don't have to raise my profile; I don't have to find a job; I don't have to help students get jobs; I don't have to help hire new colleagues; and I don't have to keep up to the minute in any area of philosophy. I go to keep in touch with things that interest me, and I go to see my friends. My scholarly impact is indistinguishable from zero. I have read no more than three or four papers in philosophy at APA meetings, and I have commented on philosophy papers two or three times. Recently, I have been on a number of panels on careers matters, but that's not scholarship.

For all that my perspective is highly atypical, I have watched the APA evolve for upward of three decades, from the beginning of my teaching career to the present. Most of the changes have been, to my mind, for the better. Here are my views of some of the big changes between then and now.

PLACEMENT AND JOB ADVERTISING

Then

There was some advertising, especially for the visible appointments at the frontline research institutions. But there was no across-the-board access to the job market. My evidence for this is only anecdotal, but I am convinced that job candidates from well-regarded graduate programs who were advised by people who knew their way around the profession had much the best of it.

Now

It's all different. We have the publication *Jobs for Philosophers* and the postings on the APA website, which are accessible to any member. Anyone, with or without department sponsorship, can apply for any job at all.

APA PROGRAM SELECTION

Then

It was said that who you were mattered in the program committees' decisions about which of the submitted papers to put on the programs and which philosophers to invite to deliver papers.

Now

The refereeing of submitted papers is all done blind. I have never served on a program committee, so I am not in a position to comment on how invited speakers are selected. However, comparing programs from the late 1960s and early 1970s with recent ones, the variety of areas of philosophy represented on programs is in general much greater. People still believe that there is less access to APA programs for some areas of philosophy and for people who work in other than the major research departments. I have no way of knowing if this is true, in general or ever, but I do think that the APA and its program committees would do well to bear in mind that (notwithstanding the gains made in widening the scope of access to its meetings programs) this criticism continues to be heard.

CONSTITUENCIES HEARD IN THE APA

Then

In 1968, the APA's membership list contained around three thousand names, including associate members. By 1971, in which year there was only one class of member, there were approximately forty-two hundred members. Insofar as the number of members reflects the diversity of the membership, a lot has happened.

Now

There are more than eleven thousand members of the APA. And since the Pluralist Revolution of the 1970s and 1980s, the view that the APA is run by and for one or two constituencies has been much reduced. Access to APA committees that shape APA programs and committee membership, as well as the nominating and program committees, is much more open than it used to be. For all that, making sure that the APA is representative of the profession of philosophy is a job without end. Again, I depend only on anecdotal evidence, but it does appear that there are constituencies who feel underrepresented and even disenfranchised. Here, appearances matter just as much as the facts of the matter, and I think we need to remember that there are still people in philosophy who feel left out or excluded by the APA.

INTERVIEWING

Then

Sometimes on campus, sometimes in odd corners of meetings hotels, sometimes in the interviewers' bedrooms.

Now

Sometimes on campus, sometimes in odd corners of public spaces in hotels, in interviewers' suites with several people present, and in designated interview spaces set up for placement. Never, never, never in bedrooms. Or hardly ever that we hear about. The interview space sometimes leaves a lot to be desired. It has sometimes been crowded, or noisy, or too far from the areas in which sessions occur. But the provision of such space is a great improvement in the way interviewing is done.

DIVERSITY

Then

In 1971, there were four standing committees: Lectures, Publications, and Research; International Cooperation; Placement; and Status and Future of the Profession. The committee on the Status and Future of the Profession had subcommittees on Participation of Blacks in Philosophy, on Opportunities for Teaching Philosophy in Two-Year Colleges, and the Status of Women in the Profession. In addition, there were Special Committees on Freedom for Latin American Philosophers and on the Defense of Professional Rights for Philosophers. Surely there were additional efforts to make the APA accessible to members of various minorities and underrepresented constituencies.

Now

The APA now has six standing committees. As in 1971, the chairs of the standing committees serve ex officio on the APA's Board of Officers. The four standing committees from 1971 survive, with the Placement Committee reconstituted in 1977 as the Careers Committee. The two additional standing committees are Teaching of Philosophy and a new standing committee on Inclusiveness. In addition, there are stand-alone committees on Blacks in

Philosophy; Defense of Professional Rights; Hispanics in Philosophy; Status of Lesbian, Gay, Bisexual, and Transgender People in the Profession; Status of Women; Asian and Asian American Philosophers and Philosophies; and the Status of American Indians in Philosophy—all of which deal in one way or another with inclusiveness. (The APA has other committees as well: Philosophy and Computers, Philosophy and Law, Philosophy and Medicine, and Pre-College Instruction in Philosophy.) Calls for nominations to these committees are circulated by mail to the membership at large. I certainly hope that all this increased APA attention to diversity in its activities and that membership will have positive results. So far, so good. But as to the future, history will be our judge.

I never seriously believed that in my career in philosophy I had any complaint about discrimination against me. (Not so on Wall Street, I have to say.) Two or three instances of seriously improper treatment regarding my progress as a graduate student, yes, but nothing that tied to my gender or to any other factor that is among those often fingered as the source of discriminatory treatment. Discrimination in my *favor* on account of gender? Yes. More than once I got a call from someone in a philosophy department who more or less said, "I hear you're a woman. Want to apply for our job in . . ." what turned out to be some area of philosophy in which I was totally unqualified.

One reason that I wasn't particularly ready to notice discrimination has to do with my upbringing. I was raised in the orthodox, New York City, red-diaper tradition: I had lefty parents; mine was a single-parent household for all but the first six or seven years of my life; I went to a progressive school through the eighth grade; and I went to summer camps with left-wing reputations. My father, when he was a part of the household, used to play me "The Ballad of Joe Hill," sung by Paul Robeson, as a lullaby. For all that, I was never much of a political activist.

Part of the red-diaper mind-set was the view that people are much more similar than they are different. Girls were not, in general, treated materially differently from boys. I never felt tracked or profiled in high school, either. About a third of the students in my school were girls, I was one of only two or three girls among dozens of boys in most of my high school classes, especially the ones in math and science. In fact, for two years, I was the only girl in math. Surely gender-based expectations were applied to people, but I never felt that I particularly suffered from them.

Another reason that I had not particularly felt discrimination is my marriage to a well-known, successful philosopher whose career thrived from day one and who was gainfully employed (or supported by a fellowship big enough for us both to live on) continuously, from the day we were married until the day he died. Philosophy was a part of the household. It's not as if we had sustained any serious philosophical discussions very much, especially after I changed careers. People used to ask what we discussed at breakfast. I suppose they hoped to hear something like "well, today, while we were enjoying our spinach and smoked salmon omelets, we resolved how to deal with the arrangement of indiscernible possible worlds in logical space" or "we finally figured out how the transcendental unity of apperception works." Instead, over the grapefruit juice and corn flakes, it was just the usual sort of breakfast conversation.

For these reasons, and maybe others, I can safely say that my career story does not support generalizations. In the APA symposium at which this chapter was delivered, several constituencies were represented. Mine was surely "etc."

NOTES

This paper grew out of a presentation at an APA anniversary symposium, "On being Black, Gay, Latino/a, Female, Asian, etc. in Philosophy before the Era of 'Diversity'" at the Pacific Division of the APA in March 2001. I owe thanks to the other symposiasts—Jorge Gracia, Gary Mar, David Hull, and Howard McGary—and to several people who offered discussion from the audience. I am grateful to Philip Kitcher, who also provided several helpful comments. I am greatly indebted to Linda Alcoff, who chaired the symposium, for her role as chair and for her encouragement and patience with this chapter.

7

What's a Brown Girl like You Doing in the Ivory Tower?

Or, How I Became a Feminist Philosopher

Uma Narayan

All autobiographical narratives involve tricky choices about where to begin or end and what to include. Difficult issues include how to write about oneself without being overly narcissistic, how to write about unfamiliar contexts in ways that are both evocative and intelligible, and how to convey the odd mixture of gratitude and criticism one has about the persons and contexts that have shaped one's intellectual life. Of course, there are also serious questions about what one feels comfortable talking about and the level of detail one wishes to share. The narrative that follows certainly lacks the candor that would obtain if I were talking to close friends about my intellectual and professional life; however, for this context, I have tried to include what I thought was interesting and important, without going into details when I did not feel comfortable doing so.

A good part of my earlier schooling took place in Uganda, where I lived between the ages of eight and fourteen. The last three of these years, I went to an all-girls boarding school, run by Irish Franciscan nuns, but where most of the teachers were lay persons, mostly Irish and English, with a few Americans and a few Ugandans of both African and Indian descent. The majority of the students were Ugandans of African descent, with a sprinkling of Asians. I had some wonderful teachers there, who encouraged my proclivity for reading widely and who introduced me to an odd range of things, from English literature and poetry, to the history of Irish nationalist resistance to British rule, to the texts of Fabian socialism, and to the popular works of Bertrand Russell. They fostered my love of reading, my pleasure in language, and they gave me a rich sense of myself as able to appreciate and criticize ideas, and to have ideas of my own. These were the years I began to take myself seriously as an intellectual due to the teachers who were willing to indulge and not ridicule

my bookish precociousness and pretensions. I fantasized myself growing up to become a teacher, although my imagination did not extend at this time beyond the possibility of teaching in a school.

These wonderful years at boarding school ended with chilling abruptness, when Idi Amin decided to "expel the Asians" from Uganda in 1973. I have repressed a good deal about that scary time, but I do remember discussions with fellow students about our safety in an all-girls school in an isolated setting, when armed militia were wandering around doing as they pleased. I remember a few of us huddling around a radio to hear that the chief justice, whose daughter was one of our former classmates, had been executed. I remember that my father was on a business trip to West Africa when the expulsion was announced, and I remember my mother panicking on the phone because she did not know where our passports or our monetary assets were—and I also remember my vowing to myself that when I was grown, I would always know where such vital entities were. I remember the quiet terror of the various military checkpoints we had to pass through on the way to Entebbe Airport when we eventually left. We were exceptionally fortunate in that my father was a wage-earning professional with no serious assets in the country and in that we were Indian passport holders, who had no problems returning to India. People of Indian origin who had British passports were allowed to emigrate to England only after extensive racist efforts to keep them out had failed, and those who were Ugandan nationals were resettled in a variety of countries as United Nations refugees. I would hardly want to argue that living through political upheavals contributes to one becoming a political philosopher, but I cannot help registering how many of the issues I think about as a philosopher—the uses and misuses of state power, citizenship, immigration, the politics of race, the gendered consequences of political instability, and colonialism and its postcolonial aftermaths—forcefully figured in this situation.

After returning to India, I finished school and entered an undergraduate college in Bombay. It was difficult not to realize that access to a college education was a great privilege, in a context where millions lacked access to basic education and literacy skills and where women were disproportionately represented among them. I was fortunate to be the daughter of an urban middle-class family, in which both sons and daughters had taken schooling for granted and were expected to aspire to a college education. For many women of my mother's generation, middle-class status made college education possible, even as dominant norms continued to make it unrespectable for them to work outside the home. I was part of the first generation of women in my family who could imagine a college education as a path to an independent career, and not simply a preliminary to marriage. When I began college, I believe I had ideas of majoring in either literature or history. The possibility of studying philosophy did not cross my horizons until I got to college, and the reasons that pushed me toward it were not only its intrinsic charms, but also my experience of yet another political upheaval.

My first year as an undergraduate was the year in which Indira Gandhi, then the prime minister of India, declared a national emergency that was to last for two and a half years, plunging a country that was used to the political amenities of a parliamentary democracy into a period of acute state repression and dictatorship. Suddenly, newspapers were censored, and people were arrested for expressing political opinions. Anyone engaging in political opposition could be arrested and indefinitely detained without ever being officially charged. The rights to assemble meetings and demonstrations no longer existed. Numerous forms of state-sponsored violence were unleashed against different groups of people—two of the most notable being the forced sterilization of men carried out in the name of family planning, and the bulldozing of slums in many urban areas.

I chose to major in philosophy because I happened to be in a class where the chair of the philosophy department, James Daniel Swamidasan (an intelligent, eloquent man on the verge of retirement), combined erudite lectures on philosophy with risky public denunciation of what was taking place around us. He showed me how a passion for ideas could be intimately connected with a passion for justice and how the privileges of education carried with them political obligations to speak and work against injustice. The rest of the professors at the college carried on as if everything was normal, business as usual—as did most of the students, for whom education seemed little more than a ticket to a lucrative professional future. I saw up close how education could function both as a powerful moral stimulus and as a powerful sedative.

The national emergency rapidly politicized me and some of my close friends, and we engaged in activities such as organizing covert talks and discussion groups, putting up posters, and disseminating information—all activities that would have been pretty innocuous if we had not been in the grips of political repression. In part because opportunities for overt political activity were foreclosed, some of my friends and I decided to work with nongovernmental organizations (NGOs) in certain Bombay slums, where we assisted medical teams, taught literacy classes for children and for teenage women, and the like. These experiences made me forcefully confront the conjoint impacts of class and gender on women whose choices and life opportunities were so different from my own that we might have well been inhabitants of different planets rather than fellow inhabitants of the same city.

These experiences also resulted in my first sense of ambivalence about philosophy. On the one hand, it was not at all difficult for me to see the deep moral and political relevance of reading Socrates, Locke, Marx, and Mill as an undergraduate in Bombay, while the political repression of the national emergency unfolded around me. On the other hand, the abstractness of philosophy, and the fact that large parts of it seemed oblivious to the concrete problems in the world around me, led me to feel restive and guilty about having the privilege of an intellectual life within it. I only realized later that there was not one single piece of writing by a woman in any of my undergraduate philosophy courses, nor was there any focus on gender or on issues that afflicted the lives of women—and it astonishes me that I did not even register these facts at the time.

My decision to major in philosophy was initially treated by my family as something of a cross between a bizarre joke and a catastrophe. On the one hand, no one quite knew what philosophy was or what majoring in it amounted. On the other hand, it was quite evident to my father that philosophy was not an avenue that could lead to lucrative employment in the real world. The riskiness of philosophy as a career option might have been less distressing to my father if I had shown signs of growing into a daughter whose central life ambition was an arranged marriage. My father would have been able to imagine and help procure a secure life for such a daughter. But alas, I was a daughter who was increasingly given to critical moral and political opinions on the arrangements that structured the world around her, and I was a woman vocal about her desire for an unconventional and independent life. In my father's perspective, such an odd daughter needed an education that would enable her to provide for herself, at least until she came to her senses. Providing for oneself ideally meant a degree in engineering, medicine, or the sciences—but even my father could tell that these were not areas where my interests lay. In my father's calculus, the next best options were a degree in economics, followed by a degree in management. Philosophy was a preposterous choice, but his antipathy only served to make me more stubborn and adamant about my decision. He consoled himself by referring to me by a Tamil phrase that means "the madwoman who studies philosophy" and by complaining to relatives that I was a daughter who "refused to use her brains." It is only in retrospect that I have suspected that my father's opposition to my study of philosophy might have been even more intense if I had been a son, whose career choices ultimately mattered more than that of a daughter.

After obtaining my undergraduate degree in 1977, I decided to go to Poona, a city about two hundred miles from Bombay, for a master's degree in philosophy, to the continuing chagrin of my father. I suspect that being away from home was the strongest motivation for this decision. Several Indian women friends of mine have remarked about how the pursuit of higher education was, for many women like us, a "respectable" reason for leaving home and for deferring the pressures toward arranged marriages that tended to escalate in our twenties. My two years in Poona were a period when I came face-to-face with the extent to which caste-linked discrimination was a reality in India. Several male students from lower-caste backgrounds faced serious experiences of discrimination and marginalization while pursuing graduate work. I also came to see the degree to which caste-linked nepotism was adversely affecting some parts of Indian academia. With a few genuine exceptions, I realized I was being taught by people who really were not equipped to teach at the graduate level. In addition, there was only one woman on the faculty in philosophy, and she was fairly junior. My years in Poona led to the start of the recognition that if I were serious about pursuing a Ph.D. in philosophy, I would do well to pursue it abroad.

I returned to Bombay after receiving my master's degree in 1979, and I taught for a couple of years in an undergraduate college affiliated with Bombay University. During these years, groups working on women's issues were beginning to form in Bombay, and I was active in them. Among the issues that we sought to publicize and criticize were the rape of poor women held in police custody, dowry murders and dowry-related harassment of women, and representations of women in the media. I read some of the major texts of Second Wave feminist theory, and I began to acquire some sense of how it might be possible to do feminist philosophy. I also worked with civil liberties groups that were engaged in trying to prevent the demolition of slums, a policy that continued even after the national emergency was lifted. Mostly, we helped conduct informal censuses in slums targeted for demolition—documenting the fact that the inhabitants were not recent unemployed squatters, but had resided there for years. We also documented the fact that they had government-issued ration cards going back for years, that they were gainfully employed in the informal sector, and that some had children enrolled in local municipal schools. Progressive lawyers would use this information (sometimes successfully) to seek to obtain stay-orders against demolition. While I enjoyed my teaching, I was also restive about the fact that there was only little connection between what I was teaching and what I genuinely cared about. In the prevailing education system, that scenario continues to this day. Courses and syllabi that were set by Bombay University changed only glacially, and individual faculty had no say in the contents of their courses. In addition, the academic qualifications for teaching in colleges and universities were beginning to change toward requiring a Ph.D., and I came to the conclusion that I needed to figure out how I was going to go abroad for this purpose.

To do so was not an easy task. My family did not have any relatives settled abroad who might be sources of information. In addition, while we were middle class, we were so on the basis of a single salary, my father's wage from his employment in the managerial sector. We had no other family assets, and we certainly did not have the kind of money required to send a child for study abroad. I was attracted to the idea of going to study in the United States because the United States of my imagination was a place informed and transformed by the civil rights movement, the women's movement, and protests against the war in Vietnam. I felt sure that these sorts of concerns would have filtered into the kinds of courses that would be available to me, and I anticipated acquiring the intellectual tools and perspectives needed to do social and political philosophy in a manner responsive to the questions and issues raised by the contemporary global context. I believed I would finally be able to engage with philosophy in a way that integrated my intellectual interests and my political concerns.

I knew a few peers, all male, who were applying to U.S. universities for graduate work in engineering and the sciences. Following their advice, I went to the United States Information Service (USIS) library in Bombay, consulted the Peterson's guide to American universities, and sent off a bunch of applications to graduate programs in philosophy, based on the limited information in this guide. I made it very clear that I could not attend graduate school without financial assistance, and I felt quite pessimistic about the prospects of obtaining financial aid. While I could see why U.S. universities might provide financial assistance for Indian students who wished to work in the sciences, I worried that there was little incentive for U.S. philosophy programs to be interested enough in a foreign student to offer her substantial financial aid.

Fortunately, it turned out that I was mistaken. When I first heard back from the institutions I had applied to, it was to learn that while they thought my credentials looked good, they felt that they could not fully evaluate these credentials. I was told that I needed to take my GRE and TOEFL exams and send in the scores. I had little idea of what these tests involved, but I took them, wincing at the fact that at the prevailing rate of foreign currency exchange, each of these exams cost me a full month's salary from my teaching job! On sending in my scores, I was delighted to receive several offers of financial assistance from the U.S. schools I had applied to. Ultimately, I chose to go to Rutgers for two reasons. First, Rutgers was one of the few places that offered me a financial aid package that would cover my estimated annual expenses—and it was well-known that one was unlikely to get a student visa to the United States unless one could show this coverage. Because I lacked assets of my own, full financial coverage was crucial to my going abroad. Second, Rutgers was close to New York City, and this was a place that felt familiar to my postcolonial imagination! In retrospect, these reasons strike me as less-than-ideal ones for a student's choice of a graduate school, but I did not have any other kind of information to work with. I knew I would be the first among any of my relatives, male or female, to pursue a Ph.D. and the first to have the opportunity to seek a degree abroad. I obtained my visa, got a loan for my airfare, and came to the United States in 1983, not knowing a soul.

My life as a graduate student was both interesting and difficult. I lived in a graduate dorm the first year and made many good friends, some of whom continue to be close friends today. Because of my prior teaching experience, I was given my own class to teach right away, and I found it enjoyable to put together a syllabus and have the control over materials and assignments that I did not have teaching in India. The one thing that I realized only after I got here was the degree to which I had lost some of the privileges of middle-class status on coming here as a student. I had only my paycheck as a teaching assistant to live on, and I had no access to the help of my family to tide me over during emergencies, as I might have had at home. As a foreign national, I could not obtain loans or even get a credit card. In addition, I had to save money to go back home to visit my family every other year, a considerable strain on already slim resources. While such economic straits were no fun, I also realize that I felt less oppressed by these circumstances because all of my close friends were impoverished graduate students themselves.

My hope that the philosophy curriculum in the United States would show vivid signs of the effects of the social movements of the 1960s and 1970s turned out to be largely unfounded. While the courses I took did provide me a better grounding in philosophy than I might easily have found in India, a considerable part of the graduate work I did was not central to my own interests. Given my imagined views of what the United States was like, I was surprised by the composition of the department. There were only a handful of women faculty, and not all of them taught graduate courses. I believe only three of the classes I took for my course work were taught by women. In addition, there was only one person of color on the faculty; there was not the slightest hint of feminist philosophy in the graduate curriculum; and there was not an extensive amount of social and political philosophy either. While the department made efforts to recruit women graduate students, they were less successful in retaining them. When I entered, I was the only woman of color. The three other American women of color who joined the department when I was there, and who continue to be friends, did not stay very long. The institution of philosophy in the United States did not resemble what I had imagined it to be.

One of the most important things that happened to me at Rutgers was Alison Jaggar's becoming the first occupant of the Laurie Chair in Women's Studies in 1985. I was fortunate to be one of two graduate student participants in the second of the two seminars she conducted while being an occupant of the chair. Being in this seminar, surrounded by a roomful of feminist scholars from the region, was an empowering experience, and I learned a great deal both about how feminist perspectives might transform the interests and concerns of mainstream disciplines, and about the importance of multidisciplinary work. The seminar was to be my first, and last, institutional introduction to feminist philosophy. It meant a great deal to me since it rekindled my hope that it was possible to integrate my feminist concerns into my intellectual work, even if it would have to wait until I "grew up!" I ended up doing a not-particularly-feminist dissertation in the philosophy of law, on the legal regulation of offensive conduct, which was an area that interested me and had some bearing on real-world issues.

One benefit of being in Alison's seminar was that I became acquainted with the women's studies program at Rutgers, which was still in its relatively embryonic stages. Many of the introductory-level courses in the women's studies program were taught by feminist graduate students from a variety of departments, and I was asked to be among them. I was delighted by this opportunity, and I was particularly delighted to make the acquaintance of an interesting range of young graduate women. I ended up teaching introductory women's studies courses virtually every semester of my last four years there, alongside teaching my classes as a teaching assistant for the philosophy department. This schedule meant that I was teaching five courses a year on average, two each semester and one during the summer, without the graduate assistants to do my grading that "real" faculty had. I find it an amusing paradox that I, who had come here hoping to *learn* about feminist work, actually spent more time *teaching* feminist courses than being a student in them!

One of the less tangible benefits of being in Alison's seminar was the feeling of being taken seriously, as someone who was not a "mere graduate student" but one who had the potential to make significant contributions. It is difficult to exaggerate the power of someone's seeing you as a competent and interesting intellectual before you are in any position to do so yourself. Alison encouraged me to turn some of my responses to the themes of her seminar into an article for the anthology *Gender/Body/Knowledge*, which she and Susan Bordo put together from work done during the seminar. I was both terrified and gratified to be asked to contribute, and the terror was well worth the effort of writing the piece and the greater confidence in myself that resulted. I was also intellectually encouraged when two professors in the Rutgers philosophy department, Howard McGary and Mary Gibson, invited me to a reading group that they were participating in. My exposure to these informal intellectual discussions, and the ideas stirred by them, eventually led me to write the first article that I submitted to and published in *Hypatia*. I was lucky to have these encouraging experiences, and they sustained the confidence I needed to finish my graduate work.

I went on the job market in 1990, still ABD ("all but dissertation"), even though my dissertation was virtually done. While I knew I might have a better shot at a job if I had defended, I was worried that actually defending would alter my visa status as a foreign national, requiring me to leave now that my graduate work was done. I thought it better to postpone my defense and thereby give myself another shot at the job market. Going on the market is a stressful period in the life of any graduate student, but I had the extra anxiety of knowing that my entire ability to stay on in this country hung in the balance. I had my share of disconcerting interviews in hotel rooms, with beds dominating the space and with all-male interviewers, some of whom were sitting on the beds during the interview. I did a number of campus interviews, which were pleasant for the most part, but some did involve minor conversational interludes that I found both strange and irksome. After all, when one is a candidate for a job, it is difficult to know what response one might safely make to compliments about one's ability to speak English or to "reassurances" that one is not being considered "merely as an affirmative action candidate." The practice at the time was for job candidates to purchase their own air tickets for campus interviews and subsequently to be reimbursed for them. Unable to obtain a credit card because I was a foreign national on a student visa, I ended up having to depend on the kindness of fellow graduate students who permitted me to charge these tickets to their credit cards! It was eye-opening to register that in some of the places I interviewed at, I would have been the first tenure-track woman in the department and that in virtually every place I interviewed at, I would have been the first tenure-track person of color.

I did end up with job offers, which meant that I could now count on staying in the country and finally convince my father that philosophy could lead to a viable career! While both my parents were happy about my securing a job, my mother was saddened by the fact that I would now permanently live abroad. I must confess that I initially accepted the job offer at Vassar primarily for "geographical" reasons. Virtually everyone I was close to in this country lived in either New Jersey or New York City. Having completely disrupted my life to come here to graduate school, I was not keen on another radical dislocation. Coming to Vassar turned out to be a far better choice than I knew I was making at the time I accepted the job here. My students are intellectually motivated, socially concerned, and open to ideas. My department was not only honorable and democratic in its functioning; it was also a department where analytic and continental philosophy were taken to be legitimate endeavors, and it was one that was open to my philosophical work, addressing the concrete social issues that were my motivating passions. In addition, Vassar was institutionally committed to sustaining a number of multidisciplinary programs, including one in women's studies. Through teaching in this program, I met a number of interesting faculty outside my home department, and I had opportunities to co-teach with faculty from other disciplines, opportunities that have enriched my teaching, my scholarship, and my understanding of multidisciplinary work.

I worked on a number of articles that addressed issues pertaining to law and public policy, ranging from issues of criminal punishment, provocation, affirmative action, surrogacy, immigration law, and battered women, to laws that banned begging and sought to evict the homeless from public spaces. I wrote articles on arranged marriage, on whether "rights" were a "Western" concept, and on the difference that attention to colonialism made to feminist engagements with rights and care discourses—all of which was work that enabled me to think about issues that were pertinent to Third World feminist concerns. Many of my senior colleagues generously read and commented on my work, and gave me useful feedback during the colloquia we hold as a department. The heterogeneity of philosophical orientations in the department made me feel that my intellectual projects were legitimate, even if they did often differ in focus, style, and substance from many of my colleagues. I was lucky to meet and get to know Mary Lyndon Shanley, my senior colleague in the political science department, who was willing to read and comment on my work. Professor Shanley invited me to coedit an anthology on feminist political theory, which was published by Penn State Press as *Reconstructing Political Theory: Feminist Perspectives*. Working with an experienced senior colleague on this project was an invaluable opportunity in itself, and it also provided me the opportunity to write an essay on feminist visions of citizenship, which was included in that volume.

During my fifth year at Vassar, I got a phone call from Linda Nicholson, who was editor for Routledge's Thinking Gender series, inviting me to think about writing a book. While I felt very honored to be invited to write for a series that I greatly admired, I felt panicked and unsure as to what exactly such a book would be. I sent her rough drafts of a couple of pieces that were representatives of my trying to think about issues pertaining to "culture" in the context of Third World feminist struggles, and I also sent her a prospectus that sketched ideas for some other possible chapters, unsure as to how much sense any of it made. Linda's encouragement and enthusiasm were crucial to my decision to attempt to write the book. I was coming up for a sabbatical in my sixth year, and I ended up using it to write the book that was eventually published as *Dislocating Cultures: Identities, Traditions, and Third-World Feminism*. I did not feel that I had any clear models for the exact kind of work I had in mind, so I felt free to experiment with content, method, and style in ways I found stimulating—but I worried about how much my projects would make sense to others. I was genuinely stunned when the book won the American Political Science Association's Victoria Schuck Award for the best book on women and politics for 1997, and I have been deeply gratified that the book has been well received.

I often feel a wave of envy when I consider the range of courses, both within and outside of philosophy, that are available to my students at Vassar, and I am grateful to have the opportunities to teach a range of courses that enrich my interests. There are, however, some shortcomings to my academic life at Vassar. The teaching load is heavy, and the commitments to teaching excellence and the availability to students expected of faculty in a small liberal arts college are undeniably demanding and exhausting at times. Working with undergraduates on senior theses, extensive service on college committees, the extra burdens of pedagogic and administrative work that accompanies involvement in multidisciplinary programs all contribute to a sense of being overwhelmed during the school year. I sometimes fantasize about a job where I would have access to graduate students and have more time for my own intellectual work. But I am far from sure how many graduate departments would have *(a)* been as receptive to and supportive of the kinds of work I do as my colleagues have been or *(b)* not confronted me with the "but, is it *really* philosophy?" question that is often a response to work that deals with concrete social issues. After listening to the stories of other women in academia, both within and outside philosophy, I know I have been very lucky indeed in the overall trajectory my academic life has taken.

I realize how much I have benefited from the changes that have taken place in the overall institution of philosophy since my graduate school days. The increase in the number of women in the profession over the last two decades is noticeably visible when one attends the APA, although the relative absence of women of color in the profession still continues to be embarrassing. I remember a conversation with an African American woman who was a fellow graduate student at the time, in the aftermath of attending an APA meeting in New York. We had both been subjected to an unbelievable amount of staring by fellow professionals, which made us feel like exotic wildlife, and she had had to deal with requests for assistance by several philosophers who, despite her APA name tag, assumed she was on the hotel staff! In anger and frustration, she burst out, asking, "Why should I have to be the one to integrate the bus?" I am sorry to say that this remains a question for women of color in the profession more than a decade later, and it is one to which I have no better answer than I had earlier, which was "What choice do we have?" Until the numbers change for the better, I am afraid that the few women of color in the profession continue to bear what a friend with an ear for alliteration once called "The Brown Babe's Burden"—the burden of being constantly asked to participate in panels, conferences, and committees because legitimate concerns that women of color be represented in these sites translate into responsibilities for which there are only a few of us to shoulder. Many women of color confront these "burdens of representation" not only within their profession, but within the institutional contexts of the colleges and universities in which they work. And, as the only woman of color and often the most junior person at more panels and events than I want to remember, I have also felt the stress of the recognition that my public performance and philosophical acuity would likely be, whether I like it or not, a measure of whether "women of color can do philosophy." If there is one thing I would like to see before I retire, it is philosophy becoming a profession where a generation of women of color do not feel these huge institutional burdens of integrating the academic and philosophical bus.

Feminist philosophy has become a vibrant and internally diverse area of scholarly activity, and in the past few years, it has even entered the main program of the APA! Institutional commitments to affirmative action policies and to encouraging a diverse and multicultural curriculum have been, and continue to be, important to increasing the numbers of women and people of color in the profession. The range of efforts made by many senior women in the profession—to mentor women graduate students, to support the recruitment and tenuring of women in the profession, to create and support institutional settings where the work of women in philosophy is taken seriously, to work to change what their departments and the profession as a whole take to be serious philosophical work—continue to be crucial to making philosophy a place where women feel empowered. I hope that the discipline of philosophy will continue to change for the better in the next two decades of my life in the profession, becoming a place where many more women and people of color feel truly at home.

8

"Don't Smile So Much": Philosophy and Women in the 1970s

Martha C. Nussbaum

In one of the photo albums that I used to fill when I still thought it important to put photos into albums, I see myself in the late summer of 1972, the beginning of my fourth year of graduate school. I am standing in our little garden in the backyard of the Peabody Terrace apartments for married students at Harvard University, a garden that always looked more like a jungle, where our cat Pamina used to play at being a great cat of the wilds. I am wearing a sleeveless navy dress with a spotless white bib. The skirt is very short, but in all other respects the look is one of Doris Day respectability. I have well-cut short light brown hair. (Blondeness came later.) I am smiling. I am seven months pregnant.

Three years before, when I was a senior at NYU, and about to go for my final interview for the Danforth Graduate Fellowship—which I won—my Dean at NYU, a round old-fashioned-looking Latinist named Cooley, who wore three-piece suits and taught the *Aeneid* without giving the appearance of understanding anything about either *amor* or *ira*, gave me some advice that shocked me. Don't smile so much, he said, because it gives an impression of subservience. This shocking and memorable advice was one of my first moments of feminist consciousness–raising, from a most unlikely source. At first, Cooley's suggestion offended me, for I had been brought up to think a smile an essential gesture of politeness. And yet, as I reflected, I did notice that I was smiling all the time, even when there was nothing particular to smile at. And I began to wonder, from time to time, whether that smile was not, indeed, a gesture of submission. Still, in 1972, even after three years of Harvard, I am still smiling, standing in the little garden of our married-student dwelling, in my dress-for-success maternity dress, with a small additional female person pounding away inside me.

There was a lot of radicalism at Harvard in those days, particularly in the philosophy department, but I was not a part of it. For one thing, I was just too busy doing my work and having a baby. But there were other reasons. I had left my elitist WASP background to marry into a liberal Jewish family who read I. F. Stone and *The Nation*; and I had left my high school Goldwater libertarianism to join the Democrats. But the left-wing groups of the 1970s had little appeal for me. At heart I suppose I have always been a liberal, attached to free speech, respectful debate, individual choice, and other Enlightenment values. I have always had extreme suspicion of cults and their leaders. The Progressive Labor Party, the part of the SDS that was prominent at Harvard, always struck me as a corporatist and totalitarian movement, a cult in all but name. People I knew were ordered to marry (or, as the case may be, to leave their marriages) for the sake of correct political values. People would say, quite seriously, absurd things, such as, "We are getting married to emulate the lifestyle of the workers." Children were suddenly told not to talk to some adult they loved, because that person had the wrong view on some microsliver of revolutionary politics. Every petition that began with a perfectly reasonable demand ended with a list of further demands that were not entailed by the first, and with at least one of which I always disagreed.

The PLP newspaper, called *Challenge*, quoted many people, in particular a class of oppressed workers called Painters' Helpers. But all of them talked the same Maoist jargon, suggesting to me that either they were not quoted correctly or they had been brainwashed into a kind of groupspeak. Both alternatives cast a negative light on PLP. Hilary Putnam used to sell *Challenge* on the street corner in Harvard Square. (Hilary, my dear friend, would be the first today to echo the sentiments of this paragraph.) But I never bought *Challenge* until Chris Hill, then the TA in my logic class, announced to the class that his wife had just given birth to their first child and he intended to go see her in the hospital, but he could not go until he had sold his last copy of *Challenge*. In the circumstances, I felt that the purchase was a virtuous act. (This story reveals a good deal about feminism, or its absence, in the left-wing movements of the time.) So licking stamps for Gene McCarthy seemed on the whole the kind of left-wing activity that made sense for me.

In other ways, too, I was not of my generation. I got married young, while most of my fellow graduate students were living in communes and having sex without commitment. The daughter of an alcoholic mother, I have always had a horror of chemical intoxication, and I am in the very small minority of people my age who have never used marijuana even once. I always was obsessed with fitness, for related reasons, and was running several miles a day even during my pregnancy. When the young interns came into the delivery room to interview me about the evident success of the Lamaze childbirth classes I had been taking (for I was lucky enough to have a fast easy delivery with no anaesthesia), I told them that Lamaze was for wimps, and running was the key. So I have always been something of an outsider, and, like most runners, a loner. The world of radical left-wing solidarity was, in so many ways, not made for me, nor I for it.

Feminist movements came along somewhat later than the SDS, but, although they were often reacting against the sexism of left-wing men, they often struck me as equally dictatorial. People were told what clothes were correct and what were not. (Skirts were out, pants were in, even if the pants were extremely tight and revealing, and worn with a halter top.) They were told what sort of teaching was compatible with correct values and what was not. Although it was at one time a common view in SWIP (Society for Women in Philosophy) that women would do philosophy differently from the way men did it, more cooperatively and less destructively, the women of SWIP could be extremely destructive. My friend and fellow graduate student Eunice Belgum came to Harvard from St. Olaf College in Minnesota, and from a conservative clerical family. Dazzled by the brilliance of fast-talking East Coast graduate students, and eager to join their bohemian radical way of life, she came to depend too much on the approval of SWIP. One day around 1975, while teaching at William and Mary, depressed for many reasons, Eunice killed herself. Shortly before, she had been denounced in a SWIP meeting for co-teaching a course on the philosophy of sex roles with a male colleague. Her parents followed up the phone calls listed as having been made on the day of her death. They found that the calls were all to students in that course, apologizing for having corrupted their consciousness by teaching with a man. I wrote the last chapter of *The Fragility of Goodness* thinking about Eunice, and gave it as a lecture in her memory at St. Olaf. I used Euripides' *Hecuba* to argue that the possibility of trust is an essential prerequisite of any political community, and indeed of decent human relations. In that way, too, I have always been a liberal.

So, out of my mistrust of the radical left, I came more slowly than some to feminism. But Harvard, in the vanguard of sexism then as now, did a lot to prod me. As I recorded in *Cultivating Humanity*, my career as a graduate student (in classics) at Harvard began when a noted Roman historian took all us new graduate students up to the roof of Widener Library, and, with a broad sweep of his aristocratic arm, showed us all the Episcopal churches that could be seen from that vantage point. I learned the anti-Semitism of the classics department very quickly, from the snide comments about my change of name from Craven (on my application) to Nussbaum (at the time of arrival), and by the rude treatment typically given my husband, a graduate student in linguistics. Its sexism I learned more slowly, watching how women were never recommended to jobs at the top universities, even though they sometimes got those jobs anyway, proving that it was false that "Yale would not hire a woman"; watching how Emily Vermeule, hired to fill Radcliffe's one tenured faculty position, a chair reserved for a woman, was treated rudely by her colleagues; learning that women could eat lunch in the Harvard Faculty Club only if they used the side dining room; watching the vilification and the firing of Caroline Bynum and Janet Martin, two first-rate female scholars who formed the first faculty women's group at Harvard. But a big moment in my transition came right around the time of that smiling photo.

In 1972 I became the first woman to be a junior fellow in the Society of Fellows, an organization modeled on the Prize Fellowships at Trinity College, Cambridge; it gives young people three years at good pay to embark on interdisciplinary careers, free of any further official degree requirements. The society had a long tradition of misogyny, going back to one of its leading figures, the classicist Arthur Darby Nock, who refused even to allow women to be invited in as guests. As the first woman to breach the tradition in the sense of full inclusion, I was welcomed with both respect and warmth by Nobel Prize–winning economist Wassily Leontief, a true feminist, who also created a child-care stipend for me, promising me that the same support would be given to male fellows who needed child care. (Leontief left Harvard shortly after, in protest over its denial of tenure to two left-wing economists.) Right after my election, I got a letter of "congratulation" from a leading Latinist in the Harvard department, one of my teachers. He said that it was difficult to know what to call a female fellow, since "fellowess" was such an awkward term. Perhaps, he opined, the Greek language could solve the problem: since the Greek for "fellow" is *hetairos*, I could be called a *hetaira*. *Hetaira*, however, as both he and I well knew, was the Greek term for courtesan, or high-class prostitute.

Here we see the real difficulty of feminism in the academy. It is the difficulty that John Stuart Mill long ago correctly identified: most men are simply not prepared to live with women on a basis of equality. They may think and maintain that they are, but their human development is paltry and does not sustain such good intentions as they may have. They have learned deviously infantile ways of perceiving women, and these ways always inflect their dealings with women as graduate students and colleagues. Men's ways of being infantile vary. Some are flirtatious and silly in a relatively harmless way. Some fear old age dreadfully, and believe that continual exercises in seduction will produce something like erotic immortality. Some long to tell you in no uncertain terms that you are a whore, because it makes them feel power. Some hate themselves and have contempt for any woman who is nice to them. Some—and these are the worst, I think—are satanic, by which I mean that they have an emptiness at their core that they fill with exercises in domination, which they market with a frequently dazzling charm. (For many years, philosophical life at Harvard was dominated by such a man, despite the utter paltriness of his philosophical contribution.) Some take no stand on any of these issues, like Dante's souls in the vestibule of hell, waving their banner now this way and now that. They don't really like what Satan does, but it seems to them excessive to say that he is bad.

There are also the good and decent men. I have the good luck in life to be drawn romantically to these types and not to the others, no doubt because of the formative influence of a father who was strong and daring, but also kind and devoted, and who sought equal strength and daring in me. I also prefer decent men as friends; I find the other types exceedingly boring. Among the good and decent men, some are unprepared for the surprises of life, and their good intentions run aground when confronted with issues like child care, housework, and women's fame. These men do better as friends than as spouses. (My husband, whom I deeply loved, and who is still one of my greatest friends, was such a man, at that time; after the birth of our child our marriage gradually became an unhappy one.) A few, like my dear friend John Stuart Mill, are ready to think in truly unconventional ways and to be a different sort of man. (For I cannot help thinking of Mill as my friend when I read his surprising letters and works.)

I got my Ph.D. in classics, and thus, although I spent a lot of time in the philosophy department, I was there primarily to work with my thesis advisor, of whom more later. I believe that the sexism of that department at that time was less extreme and less universal than that of the classics department, but real all the same. More generally, the philosophical academy contains all the types of men that life contains, with the qualification that philosophy selects for proud, quick-talking, dominant personalities and against the gentle and quiet. The main problem of feminism in philosophy is the infantile level of human development of many of the men who are in it. This problem will not change without large-scale social changes that are still in their infancy. The most we can do is to deter the worst abuses and punish them when they occur, meanwhile trying to bring up young men who think differently, and women who assert their dignity.

Often, finding myself adrift in a world that admired me but treated me with the crudeness that the *hetaira* story illustrates, I found that my life went better if I threw in my lot with other outcastes. I learned early that gay men are frequently more perceptive and more truly feminist than straight men, with more of the friendship that professional women seek and less of the anxiety about eroticism that becomes so tedious to deal with. They also have an invaluable critical "double consciousness" of the outsider about maleness and its ways; and they have learned to see the whole business of gender as a way of replicating social hierarchy. I owed much of my sanity, early in my career, to the friendship of Glen Bowersock, in the Harvard Classics Department (who unfortunately left Harvard a little before my tenure decision), and, later, of David Halperin, eminent scholar and one of the primary founders of gay studies, and of John J. Winkler, the classical scholar who, along with

Catharine MacKinnon, waged the first fight over sexual harassment at Yale University in 1975.

But since the topic has been mentioned, let us now, indeed, consider sexual harassment. There is a tendency today for young women to think of policies against sexual harassment as both unnecessary and constraining. They feel condescended to, when they are told whom they may and may not sleep with. Rational adults should be able to sort these things out their own way, and if women stand up for themselves they will not be hurt. I suppose I used to think this way, too, back in the days of excessive smiling. Let me try to explain why I no longer do.

My thesis advisor, G. E. L. Owen, was a brilliant scholar of ancient Greek philosophy. He was also an alcoholic and an attempted womanizer. A Welshman who struggled to assert his stigmatized lower-middle-class Welshness against the elite British academic society that condescended to him, he viewed it as an essential part of his manly honor to attempt to sleep with every woman who came his way. This prominently included all female graduate students, one after the other. The typical pattern was as follows. (I have compared stories with others.) You had an appointment with Owen. Arriving late, he said he had left your paper, or chapter, at home. Then, if it was Cambridge, England, where the workroom was also the home, he would pour sherry, offer some to you, put on a record, and start talking about the sadness of life. If it was Harvard, where the workroom was several blocks from the home, he would try to convince you to come home to find and discuss the allegedly forgotten essay. But even if you said no, he would still produce sherry, and begin to talk about the sadness of life. Much though you tried to return the topic to Aristotle, he would go further into sentimental weltschmerz. You would know that seduction was at hand when two things happened. First, he played Darius Milhaud's "Le Boeuf sur le Toit," to show how lively, funny, and virile he was. Second, he recited Auden's "Lay Your Sleeping Head, My Love," in order to show you how sad he was about age and time. At this point he would put his arm around you, grab a breast, and see what happened next. There were a couple of variants. One time when I stayed overnight in a Cambridge college guest room, he walked into my room at 8 A.M. and simply lay down on top of me, an act that in some sense I count as an attempted rape, although his physical weakness allowed one to push him away quite easily.

Now this was far from being the worst thing in sexual harassment. For Owen did not retaliate against women who said no, even repeatedly. He thought he had salvaged his honor by attempting, but such was his self-contempt that he thought all the better of those who would not have him. Only those who said yes got hurt—by being drawn into the misery of his alcoholic life, by becoming responsible for getting him out of bed and into class in the morning, by becoming the targets of gossip and criticism, and by becoming the targets for his own self-hatred, as he relentlessly belittled them in class. One day Julia Annas and I were sitting in the seminar room before class making fun of D. H. Lawrence, and the current mistress walked in, pale, exhausted, and depleted. Hearing only the name of Lawrence, "Oh Lawrence," she exclaimed in a sad wispy voice. "Aren't his novels wonderful?" We felt so sad, Julia and I, thinking of the fantasy she must have been enacting. (Now I actually do think that Lawrence's novels are wonderful, but I still don't think this young woman's life was.)

Even Owen's relatively benign pattern of sexual harassment, though, created an atmosphere in which women simply had no dignity, and were unable to assert it. One of my fellow graduate students, more political in those days than I, did protest to the chair of the philosophy department, who was embarrassed and had no idea what to do. At that public complaint, Owen hit the roof, and refused to work with her henceforth. To this day, she suffers professionally from that early exclusion. I thought at the time that she had overreacted, since one could handle it by simply saying no. And I did, again and again. I admired Owen enormously, and I also felt sorry for him. Just as I never accused my mother of being drunk, even though she was always drunk, so I managed to keep my control with Owen, and I never said a hostile word to him. I knew I would never sleep with him, and that I would go on working with him, and that he would not turn against me.

But that was really not adequate. The woman who complained was right and I was wrong. For my dignity was always compromised, by being forced to be available for the Milhaud/Auden ritual, albeit with a negative ending. And the general idea was created, in that circle, that women were there as sexual objects. Even though I was Owen's star pupil, I remained denuded of dignity. One day Bernard Williams took a walk with me along the backs behind King's College, Cambridge, and said, you know, there is a price you are paying for this support and encouragement. Your dignity is being held hostage. You really don't have to put up with this. I understood his point, but I didn't deeply feel it: I felt in control of the situation. So things went on as before. Although after Owen's return to England from Harvard I managed to avoid, for the most part, situations in which the ritual could enact itself, I still worked with him and even, while an assistant professor, coedited a Festschrift for his sixtieth birthday. (We chose sixty because we suspected he would not live to sixty-five; he died a few months after the Festschrift party.) My coeditor, a male scholar at Cambridge, kept saying to me, "Why are we editing a Festschrift for this man? He has just been at my house for dinner, and he insulted my wife." And I would say, "Calm down, Malcolm. He is a great scholar with a very sad life." As in my earlier life, so here: my propensity has always been to put up with too much bad behavior, smiling. I feel I understand Anita Hill.

The first general thing I want to say about sexual harassment in the academy is that things are rarely this benign. Usually there is punishment afoot somewhere, and notice that even in this case, the woman who complained was sorely punished. I was punished, too, by the enmity of Owen's male students and former students, many of whom simply assumed that I was sleeping with him, and that this was why he liked my work. (And when, much later, I became a friend of the late Gregory Vlastos, then in his eighties, and he, too, liked my work, the same people assumed that I was sleeping with him, although this was not the case, and anyone who knew me at all well would have known that it was deeply unlikely.)

The second thing I want to say is that the availability of women for sex, or even attempted sex, creates an atmosphere in which women have no dignity. Men think that whatever advancement women get, they get through sex. Women are pitted against women in ridiculous and demeaning ways. Whether the favorites are the ones who say no or the ones who say yes, an in-group and an out-group are created in a seminar, and the academic endeavor is impeded thereby. This atmosphere hurts men, too, because they come to think that women have advantages they don't have. This hurts their relations with themselves, and with women.

In our law school we have a strict rule: no sex between faculty and any law student under any circumstances, not even a third-year student bound for a firm, whom you know you will never teach again. Some faculty think this is too harsh. But the female students overwhelmingly support it, because they say they do not want to sit through first-year classes and feel that they are being looked over as potential dates two years hence. They feel that even third-year dating would create a bad atmosphere from the start for all women, and I believe that they are right.

The third and most important thing I want to say about sexual harassment in the academy is that the feminist analysis of sexual harassment is correct: this is not about love, it is about power. What Owen got out of the ritual was an assertion of his virility and his power over powerless women. The fact that he could do this to young and healthy me meant, to him, that he was not as decrepit and out of control as he feared he was, and was. Many men are far less sentimental, far more sadistic, in their conception of what power involves. But even the sentimental conception of power poisons the academic environment.[1]

But what of love, you ask. Can't women search for love? And can't love within an academic program sometimes be wonderful? Of course the answer to this question is yes. Love is just as wonderful as philosophy, and a love that is combined with shared goals and intellectual passions can be the most wonderful of all. And yet, I would say that if the love is between a male faculty member and a female graduate student, it is never worth the risk. The student is too vulnerable, and there are far too many things that can go wrong.

Suppose, though, one is a senior colleague and the other is a junior colleague. Here there seems to me to be more latitude, provided that the department can construct an acceptable procedure to disqualify the senior person from voting on that person's promotion. But notice this: that even in the best case, where the relationship is wonderful and enduring, there is no breakup and no bitterness, no asymmetry of desires, you are losing a vote that might be quite important for your future, especially if the person you love, as often happens, is in an area of the subject close to your own. Moreover, you will risk running afoul of the usual prejudice and suspicion about how women get ahead: for people will think that the senior person's good opinion of you means nothing at all, is all about sex; whereas without the sex they might believe him. And if there should be any messiness at all about the matter, for example, a marriage or marriages that suffer as a result, the natural reaction will be to think that the woman is a troublemaker, and we'd rather not have her around. Men rarely perceive themselves, or their colleagues, as even part causes of trouble.

Would I, knowing these things, shape my life differently? I honestly don't know.

But are sexual harassment rules and policies any use? They are surely not perfect. For a complaint against a faculty member causes great upheaval, and if women are perceived as troublemakers when they say yes, they are so perceived in spades when they say no and blow the whistle. They also fail to catch the worst abuses. Notice that Owen's relatively benign conduct was of a piece with the incautious and emotional nature of his approach. A really sinister harasser is much more calculating, and will usually find out whether you are likely to say yes well before he has done anything overtly incriminating. The satanic types I have mentioned will thus rarely get caught, and the one I have in mind got caught, in the end, and fired from Harvard, only because he had also engaged in financial crime, which Harvard takes far more seriously than the dignity of women.

On balance, though, I think that such policies have a great informational and deterrent value. They tell the clueless, who are many, that there are problems with certain types of conduct, even if they themselves have never noticed those problems. Then, if the man is a relatively benign type, he will be deterred. Meanwhile, an atmosphere is created that affirms women's dignity. No whistle-blower will have to suffer what my friend suffered—relegation to the fringes of the graduate program, constant criticism from other students. Even if male faculty still have a hard time dealing with an accusation, she will have the institution and its public values on her side, and this is a lot.

I believe that I smiled too politely in this situation, and I now think that one should never smile when sexual harassment is afoot. One should recognize it, and name it, and publicize it, and, above all, prevent it, by education, consciousness-raising, and in general constant tiresome harping on the harms it does. It is all very well to say that women should be able to take pleasure in their sexuality and not hide it. But I fear that men are not yet ready for a world in which women's sexuality will not be held against them in some way, and held against their work. When younger men are daring and creative, doing work that challenges the traditional norms of a discipline, older men react as if a son of theirs had just won at Wimbledon. When a young woman is daring and creative in that way, not simply following the lead of her male predecessors, older men still react, far too often, as if a daughter of theirs had just taken off her dress in public. The only way to gain a respectful hearing for ourselves, and our work, and our creativity and daring, at this point in human history, is to establish that we are not primarily sexual beings. Sexual harassment rules and policies are one important step in the direction of that goal.

But in that photo I was smiling at my husband, who was holding the camera. And I was smiling at my pregnant stomach. So what of children, and their relation to a philosophical career? My daughter Rachel is now twenty-nine, a stunning dynamic individual with a mind 100 percent her own, writing a Ph.D. thesis in German cultural history. I love being with her. From the time in utero when she pounded with determined rhythm, first the fists and then the feet, she has argued with me, and I love it, and her. She was, in respect of my work, an easy child. She learned to read early, and always loved reading; she sought out her own contemplative space, and left me mine. And she was sick and home from school only an amazing one day in her entire thirteen years from kindergarten through high school.

So if the world of the philosophical academy made it difficult for me to raise Rachel, a fortiori it would be difficult for women with more than one child, or children who demanded a lot of attention, or children who got sick a lot, or even a normal amount. And it was exceedingly difficult. Already when I was pregnant, my thesis advisor told me story upon story of women who had babies and stopped writing philosophy. He did this out of anxiety, and with the real hope that I would both have a child and continue writing philosophy. But it imposed a stress nonetheless. Because Rachel was a small baby and I am long-waisted, I did not look very pregnant, even toward the end. I remember Owen saying repeatedly to me, "Perhaps it is a wind egg." And I think that is what he wished. I brought my Aristotle texts to the hospital, feeling that I could not stop working for even a short time without making people think I had stopped completely. I missed only one Monday night dinner at the Society of Fellows.

During the three years that I was in the Society of Fellows, however, life was very good. Leontief provided extra money for child care, and he was one of those relaxed joyful people who could relieve stress about the whole situation. (He said, "I know you'll get your work done, but I am worried that you may feel unable to enjoy the social events of the society; so I want you to have this extra money.") I found care that was, though expensive, good—first with an in-home sitter, later at the Radcliffe Child Care Center. It was when I started to teach that the problems began. My husband was teaching at Yale and I at Harvard, so we kept our Cambridge apartment and he commuted to New Haven five days a week. So, from the time we began teaching in 1975 until we separated in 1985, and after that, I was in effect a single parent. In some ways, I found, being a single parent was easier than trying to share responsibilities with my husband. For although there was more work to do, I could just do it, without the extra feeling of injustice, or the always vain and difficult efforts to get him to do what I took to be his fair share.

Still, the facts were these. School began at 8:30 and ended at noon, from preschool until third grade—when it ended at three. For afternoons she had to go to the child-care center. This meant worrying about car pools in the morning and either at noon or in the afternoon, until she was old enough to walk to a baby-sitter's house for afternoon care (around the age of ten). Car pools in those days were even more hateful than they are per se, because they not only meant being dependent on others who might prove unreliable, they also meant enduring the constant critical scrutiny of non-working mothers, who were pretending that driving the car pool delighted them and was their chosen profession. Any departure from home at any time after five required a sitter, and the logistics of lining up sitters dominated a good deal of life.

Meanwhile, in the philosophy department (where my office and my heart were, although I had a joint appointment with classics), life went on as if no children existed. Colloquia were routinely scheduled at five, after the child-care centers closed. The satanic figure held his usual evening dinner/seminar for the junior faculty from six to ten, every two weeks, and attendance was morally compulsory. It was clear that participating in these discussions of Wittgenstein, which really meant listening to him and playing various scripted roles as his interlocutors, all for his tape recorder (since he wrote nothing), was the central way in which one's philosophical ability would be assessed, and that his opinion would, as it always did, greatly shape the opinions of others—not to mention the fact that, trusted by the dean, he was also in charge of the ad hoc committees for tenure in the entire university. (His career would show a good actor how the role of Iago ought to be played.) I felt that a better way to assess my work might be to read some of it and talk with me about it. I felt it was rather as if a young basketball player was told that his skill would be assessed by seeing how he could help out in the practice sessions of an aging star tennis player. I had to find and pay a sitter every time I went to one of these things, and I would much rather have been home with Rachel. Hilary Putnam and Robert Nozick agreed with me, and brought the matter up with honest Iago. Next time we were told, "You all should understand that you don't have to come to this seminar." We interpreted this statement, correctly, as meaning that we did have to go, and we kept on going. At my tenure time, this person was not only a dogged opponent of my promotion in the philosophy department (where I got a four–three positive vote), but he also campaigned heavily against me with the classics department (where I got a five–four negative vote). Much later, after he was fired, it emerged that he and a secretary who was his mistress apparently diverted a letter from Nozick as chair that was supposed to go to the Classics Department, telling them why the philosophy department had voted in my favor, but that never arrived. I had assumed that Bob, who was out of town a lot on account of his divorce, had simply not written the letter. I should have known better.

But to return to the topic of child care, many baby-sitters, in short, were required, and it was impossible to mention the whole topic of child care, for fear of being perceived as uncommitted or unprofessional. Again, one had to smile cheerfully as if one's life were the same as any other professional's, while knowing that this was not so. I remember vividly the day this began to change. We had a visiting speaker; because the talk began at the usual 5 P.M., I had gotten a baby-sitter to pick up my daughter from day care. A few minutes into the question period, Bob Nozick stood up, and, with the carefree insouciance of which only the tenured are capable, said, "I'm sorry, I have to go now. I have to pick up my son from hockey practice." For me, this was a world-historical moment. The forbidden topic had been mentioned, as a normal part of a professional life. As always, Bob was brash, confident, and unashamed. So one need not, perhaps, be ashamed of having child-care duties. Perhaps this dual responsibility could be respected in a dignified professional world. I believe that Bob, who was in surprising ways a true feminist, raised this topic deliberately, in order to pose some questions about how well the department was treating its parents. But whether or not this was true, it gave me permission to begin getting angry at the totally inadequate arrangements for the support of child care, inside the family, in the workplace, and in the larger society.

There has, I think, been a lot of improvement in our academic lives in the area of sexual harassment.[2] In the area of child care things have changed much more slowly. I believe that men now share child-care duties somewhat more than they did before; I had three young male colleagues at Brown who really did split the job roughly fifty-fifty, and it pleased me to see little children in the office in backpacks on their father's backs. But there is less change than there should be, and in some fields, in particular law, I see a true backsliding. My colleagues who are in their forties and fifties do more child care than those in their thirties and twenties. In large part, I believe that this backsliding results from the demands of the law-firm world, which are so exorbitant that they are clearly incompatible with any family life that has home-based work in it; so young men who enter this world choose wives who say they are willing to stay at home. And women who enter it end up on a lesser "mommy" track, or remain childless. But universities are also to blame. Maternity leave is still not automatic at our university; it is given at the discretion of one's dean, and it has been refused. It is possible at many universities, including ours, for a man to apply to take paternity leave, but fewer men than women avail themselves of this possibility, because child care is still stigmatized. Work arrangements are now slightly more thoughtful about hours and their relation to duties; but only slightly. And people who complain are still stigmatized.

The problem of child care is part of a much larger problem of care labor that all modern societies are facing, especially as the population ages. To solve it, we need government programs, a new attitude toward the workplace and its demands, and more equal sharing in the home. (Nor should such programs be confined only to child care: care for elderly and sick dependents of many kinds should be included.) The academy is a relatively benign place for young women in these respects, because it offers flexible hours, and a lot of the real work can be done at home. Nonetheless, as my female graduate students get jobs and have babies—four babies among my recent or current Ph.D.'s in the past two years alone—I fear for them, and I see them facing conflicts that they should not have to face. I note that some husbands are extremely helpful, even with respect to moving to a less desirable job to eliminate a commute and share care more fully. Others are not so helpful. I see that some institutions are extremely supportive of young women who have children while untenured, and others are much less supportive. We have a long way to go to solve these problems in ways that make full professional equality possible for women who have children (or aged parents) to care for.

I have a very happy life now. My daughter is a great friend and traveling companion. I have a partner (indeed, we recently became engaged) whom I deeply love, who is one of those rare men who truly takes delight in female strength. He is also a wonderful father, and shares custody of his daughter fifty-fifty. We live in separate places, and intend to continue doing so. I think of Godwin and Mary Wollstonecraft as our examples. For me, marriage is about the celebration of love and commitment, and I feel this has little to do with sharing space. We both feel that romance is promoted by space and arranged "dates," to which we can look forward with excitement. It's easier to maintain joy and passion if togetherness is not enforced or humdrum. Others make other choices. But I know that now I am choosing, whereas before I was fitting into a predetermined formula, and convincing myself that I liked it.

Professionally, I survived my Harvard tenure rejection and have gone on to do work that I love and believe in. I had wonderful support at that time from Brown University, and I still feel enormous gratitude to Ernie Sosa, Dan Brock, and the other men in philosophy and classics who fought to hire me, and then made me feel respected and at home. Brown taught me that a university could be committed to social justice and could fight energetically against sexism. So I have moved a good way beyond the sexism that I once thought would overwhelm me. But when I was writing my 2000 presidential address for the APA Central Division, the old fears of what men would say still haunted me. I fought them, and I made a point of giving a tough feminist talk, about justice in the family and the relation between justice and care. What made me most happy was that people could hear in it an anger that I had been able to use creatively. One woman said afterward, "That was a kick-ass talk." That was among the nicest things anyone had ever said to this prisoner of politeness.

So when I say that I used to smile too much, I do not mean that women should have less joy, or that feminism should be a grim life-negating business. I have always been a joyful person, and my work has roots in the experience of joy. For my high school yearbook I chose Shelley's ode to the spirit of delight as my epigraph, and I would choose it again. What I have discovered, however, is that there is a large difference between joy and the smile that aims to please and to be what pleases; and an even larger difference between joy and the smile that conceals an anger that is too unacceptable, too feared, to be acknowledged. When I look at that photo from 1972, and ask myself what kind of smile that is, I find it impossible to say. Today, I know (most of the time, anyway) what sort of smile I am smiling—or, as the case may be, not smiling. I like my anger, and I know it is not going to kill anyone; it might actually do good. All this seems to me to be progress.

NOTES

I want to thank the following people for very helpful comments on a draft of this article: Kate Abramson, Linda Alcoff, Rachel Barney, Susan Brison, John Deigh, Michael Green, David Halperin, Barbara Herman, Michelle Mason, Rachel Nussbaum, Henry Richardson, Nancy Sherman, Geoffrey Stone, Cass Sunstein, and Leslie Williams. Needless to say, these people do not all agree with me about everything.

1. The effect on lesbian women is subtle yet highly significant. An openly lesbian woman is perceived from the start as outside the system and as confronting it in a hostile way; thus she becomes the target of male anger and discrimination. (It is for related reasons that recent legal thought has favored the idea that discriminatin against gays and lesbians is a type of sex discrimination: it is all about shoring up the

hierarchy of power by enforcing a heterosexuality in which women, and their sexuality, are controlled by men. See Andrew Koppelman, *The Gay Rights Question in Contemporary American Law* (Chicago: University of Chicago Press, 2002).

2. I note that among the readers of this piece who offered comments on this point, about half say that things have actually changed less than I suggest, and about half say that things have gotten much better. This difference suggests the great importance of a local culture of proper behavior in shaping women's experiences.

9

At the Feet of Mrs. Ramsay

Andrea Nye

Is there a moment when a woman's mind comes to life? A moment in which an unrealized potentiality becomes a possible future? Perhaps the precipitating factor is attending a particular school, working with a gifted teacher, or reading a provocative book. If there was such a moment in my own young life, it was a painful encounter with a teacher—Miss Grant I will call her—whose pedagogical style owed little to arms-length professionalism.

It was my senior year in high school. The year before I had been plump and shy. I played the cello in the school orchestra and seemed constantly to stumble as I carried my large and clumsy instrument to and from school. Like Alice's body in Wonderland, mine was playing bewildering tricks on me—bleeding, flushing, and swelling with little advance notice. A year later, an amazing metamorphosis took place; I was now gaunt and shy. My hair, long and shaggy the year before, was cut and permed, putting a small-cropped head on my newly slim shoulders. My hormone levels had stabilized. For the first time, sexuality was more enticing than it was overwhelming.

I went to an all-girls school in the Philadelphia suburbs. In this rarefied feminine enclave, we communicated with the opposite sex rarely, seeing boys only at occasional chorus concerts and chaperoned parities. Romance was limited to pictures in magazines over which we developed passionate crushes. Real life was Latin verses with Miss Eldridge, French translation with Mademoiselle, algebra from Miss Main, and, most important for me, literature with Miss Grant.

We wore uniforms: in the warmer months, cotton dresses in pastel colors; in the winter months, gray flannel skirts and white shirts. Makeup and jewelry were forbidden. A trace of lipstick, a dangling bracelet, a shoe with too high a heel was ruled out of uniform and thus earned one an immediate

demerit. Our teachers were stolid and strict. They wore mannish suits. They were unmarried and lived in pairs. They looked at us balefully over wire-rimmed spectacles. Lack of preparedness, inattention, and slow-wittedness were viewed with resigned disappointment.

Miss Grant, however, was different. Simple denseness she ignored, perfunctorily grading the slower girl's themes without comment. She concentrated on a chosen few, and with these few her disappointment was neither mild nor resigned. One of her frozen silences could poison one's life for days. I cannot say that I worshipped Miss Grant the way some girls worship a favorite teacher. I might have, except for the fact that I could never, even years later, step back sufficiently from what happened between us to see her as an object. Instead, she became a substanceless point of aspiration, not because she had any power over me beyond the occasional bad grade, but because of the quality of her judgments. The other adults in my life, preoccupied with their own tangled affairs, paid little attention to me beyond reprimands for the occasional bad conduct. Miss Grant lived for the girls she taught. As a result, in the place of platitudes and honesties, her judgment tolerated no placating excuses. Sharp, one-sided, even brutal, her pronouncements had the authority of passion. The few of us whom she singled out for special favor lived in dread of her often harsh comments on our work, but we also waited eagerly for the next conference when under her auspices we would continue our initiation into the life of the mind.

I had reached the inner circle of her chosen students well before the September of my senior year. I came back to school after summer vacation ready to claim the prerogatives of graduation. After humiliating early years in the public school system—in which my mind had been simultaneously numbed by the taunts of cheerleaders and future prom queens, and lulled to sleep with rote learning—my intelligence had revived. I was liked and encouraged by my teachers. I had a popular circle of friends. There was a good chance I would be accepted at an Ivy League college. Most important of all, Miss Grant thought my work had promise. The hot September sun, the laziness of early fall, the tips of the leaves turning crimson were omens of success to come. For the first time, I felt a sense of power. I felt I could take my life up in my hands, shape it, and make it what I wanted it to be regardless of whatever wintry chills that might be coming. To my parent's dismay, I gave up the cello, never again took it out of its threadbare brown serge case. Newly unencumbered, I arrived at school with uniform unrumpled and dignity intact.

Miss Grant's class was first period. Fifteen of us walked into her classroom that September, the advanced English class. Miss Grant hardly glanced as we filed in; she only sat at her desk leafing through some papers. Once we were seated, she looked up, then braced herself for fresh banalities that might have infected us over the summer. Light from a bank of small-paned windows etched deep lines into her brow. After some preliminaries she announced, "Girls, this term we are going to read Virginia Woolf."

She looked out at faces framed by the tightly crimpled hair in fashion at the time, her eyebrows slightly raised. I imagined her thinking, "I mean some of us are—the rest of you don't look capable of reading anything more challenging than Grace Metalious." I blushed. I myself was deep into the best-seller *Peyton Place*.

Miss Grant went on, "The name of the book is *To the Lighthouse*. Some of you have probably already bought it from the bookstore." She looked around the room.

Yes. On most of our desks was a small paperback with a woodcut representation of Lily Briscoe painting at her easel on the cover. Behind Lily on the open sea floated the sailboat that would take James and the others to the lighthouse. I sniffed its pages, doubtful that there could be anything very interesting inside so prosaic a cover.

"We will begin by reading the first twenty-five pages for tomorrow," Miss Grant told us. "In the meantime I'm going to tell you something about the author, Virginia Woolf." Miss Grant got up from her desk. She walked to the small-paned windows. Looking out over the lawn, she told us about Woolf's life, her literary circle, her husband, her struggle with depression. "In the end, she committed suicide," she finished flatly.

Half attending up to then, we started awake. Death, like sex, was seldom mentioned in our company. Worse, Miss Grant's voice had become slightly hoarse and choked with emotion. "She made a choice. It was her illness. It kept getting worse. She thought if she went on she would go mad."

We squirmed in our seats. Wasn't it an infringement of good manners to expose one's emotion in this way? We longed for the bell to ring and announce the end of the class, but there were still some heavy moments of silence to be endured as Miss Grant stood at the window and thought about Virginia Woolf—putting rocks in the pocket of her coat and throwing herself into the river while Leonard waited for her to come up for lunch from the cottage where she wrote in the mornings. Of course, she didn't come and never came. Finally, he went down the flagstone path to find her walking stick floating on the surface of the water. Mercifully, the bell rang.

The next few weeks, we read *To the Lighthouse* with Miss Grant. If they had paid attention to such things, our parents no doubt would not have thought it a suitable book for young girls. I still have the copy we read, marked with many of Miss Grant's comments, which I penciled into the margins. When I take it down from my bookshelf, I am back in Miss Grant's class again, visiting at the sea with the Ramsay's. Through all the difficulties of Woolf's modernist stylistic prose, Miss Grant brought the house and its occupants to life: Mrs. Ramsay, the beautiful angel of the house looking out at the glittering sea; her unruly children; and most important for my future, the philosopher, Mr. Ramsay, accepting homage, contemplating the nature of reality, and relying on his wife and children for comfort and reassurance.

Page by page we read. "What about this student of Mr. Ramsay's, Charles Tansley?" Miss Grant asked one day. We leafed through our books trying to recollect who this could be, Charles Tansley was a doctoral student of Mr. Ramsay and a minor and unsympathetic figure. Certainly, he did not have the charisma of his mentor, and he played little part in the charged sexual atmosphere that surrounded Mr. Ramsay. Nor was he anyone with whom the spinster painter Lily Briscoe with her little puckered face might yet find romance. He was writing a dissertation on the "influence of something on somebody." He wore ill-fitting clothes and talked about the working class.

We kept our eyes cast down, trying to avoid attention.

Miss Grant tapped one blunt finger on the desktop. "Well? Are we awake yet this morning, after the weekend's festivities?" Her lips curled slightly at the thought of our puerile amusements.

"No one likes him," someone blurted out.

Heads turned. It was Cathy, a scholarship student. Her father was a postman. She had made few friends among these upwardly mobile daughters of lawyers, doctors, and businessmen. She was a diligent student. She recited Latin translations by heart. She knew the rules of French grammar. She never made mistakes in computation. She always remembered the names of minor characters in novels. But she never seemed to be able to say the right thing or say it in the right way. Nothing came easy for her; no flights of fancy helped her along, no bursts of creativity lightened her effort, only hard plodding labor.

"Cathy. Enlighten us." Miss Grant turned to Cathy.

Prodded, Cathy made a faltering attempt, repeating one of Mrs. Ramsay's offhand remarks. "He's a bore."

Miss Grant's eyebrows rose.

"He follows Mr. Ramsay around. Mrs. Ramsay, too, just trying to get them to like him."

"And why exactly to you think he needs to do that?" Miss Grant had her killer look as she contemplated Cathy, who was nervously twisting a piece of straggling brown hair round and round on finger, straining to come up with an acceptable answer.

"He's a . . . he's a prig."

Miss Grant did not relent. "And why is he a prig?"

After some more hair twisting, Cathy got out a few more words. "Because he only thinks of how people are going to look at him?"

"And his family, his class? The fact that his father was a druggist? That his family didn't read books or go to museums like the aristocratic Mrs. Ramsay and her children? I would think that you, you of all people, might have noticed some of that," snapped Miss Grant.

Now it's true that we had not befriended Cathy as we might have; it is true that behind her back sometimes we made fun of her awkwardness. Still, we had never been overtly cruel to her, and we knew that what Miss Grant said was cruel. We winced at Cathy's pale paralysis as she slowly digested what Miss Grant had said. Another girl might have run out of the room in tears. Cathy just sat. Miss Grant could not have hoped that some day she would be one of her protégés, but she did not soften as she contemplated the inevitable result of her remark. Nor did it occur to any of us to stand up in protest or walk out like a class-conscious member of Charles Tansley's working class might have done. What we did do was go home to read again, about Tansley's walk to the village with Mrs. Ramsay and about Mrs. Ramsay's condescension as she accepted the homage of her husband's disciple and listened inattentively to his discourse on class struggle.

We read on. I was intrigued by Mr. Ramsay. What was this important-sounding subject, metaphysics, that had given him such fame, that accounted for the admiration of Tansley and the others. I contemplated his son's answer to Lily Briscoe's questions about the nature of Mr. Ramsay's "important contribution": "Subject and object and the nature of reality."

I meditated on Mr. Ramsay's vision of an ideal thought ordered like the keyboard of a piano, from *A* to *B* to *C*, and on to *Z*. How heroic that would be, I thought. How clear.

I looked forward more than usual to my monthly conference with Miss Grant. I hoped she would be impressed with my interest in philosophy, and I had just turned in a paper I was proud of.

The assignment had been to explain the significance of the character Lily Briscoe. My prose was flowing smoothly. I was past the embarrassment of spelling or grammar mistakes. I thought that I had achieved a certain eloquence on the sadness of Lily's single life. I thought I described accurately the contrasting richness of Mrs. Ramsay's life: Mrs. Ramsay, whom Lily so much admired; Mrs. Ramsay, who admired her husband as he wove, as she put it, "the admirable fabric of the masculine intelligence"; Mrs. Ramsay, who gave elegant dinner parties, who inspired the love, even the adoration of men on account of her beauty. In contrast, Lily, as far as I could see, with her "little Chinese eyes" was a starving child at a sweetshop window.

The afternoon of the conference I walked up the steps to Miss Grant's office with confidence. She would make me tea, Earl Grey tea with its exotic foreign flavor. Together we would savor the fruits of my intelligence and sensitivity. On the desk before her was my paper. I sat down expectantly. There was a moment of silence.

Slowly and deliberately, Miss Grant picked up the paper and handed it to me. "Don't ever hand anything like this in again. It's nonsense. It's worse than nonsense. I suggest you go back and this time actually read the book, from the beginning."

My eyes filled with tears. I was stunned. I had not expected anything like this. "Just like Cathy, stupid Cathy," I couldn't help thinking. Tongue-tied, I sat in frozen misery.

"We will say no more about it."

Summarily, I was dismissed. I stumbled out.

For days, I was on the verge of tears, all my newfound confidence destroyed. I determined never to go back to school. I would drop out and get a job in a shop. I told myself that Miss Grant, a spinster like Lily Briscoe, was blinded by her own failed life. I briefly considered reporting her to the head mistress as an abusive teacher. Life went on. I went to school. I did my work. One day, a week or so later, when we had almost finished reading *To the Lighthouse*, Miss Grant called me back after class. "Oh Andrea, I think you are going to like what we are reading next, *The Brothers Karamazov.*"

That very evening, I was deep into Dostoyevsky's unwieldy masterpiece. I was thunderstruck by the Grand Inquisitor's indictment of theology. I played with my first philosophical puzzle: how can you reconcile the idea of a good and omnipotent god with the existence of evil. I sympathized with Ivan's intellectual crisis. I remarked—yes, by then I did manage to remark—the difference between Ivan's torment and Mr. Ramsay's academic success.

The truth is that from the beginning, through all my resistance and hurt feelings, I had known that Miss Grant was right. I had not read *To the Lighthouse* with care. I had not grappled with the reality of women's lives depicted there. I had not understood the subtlety of Woolf's criticism. Instead, I had superimposed on her book images from *Ladies' Home Journal*. When I could bear it, I tormented myself with the sickening realization of how it must have disgusted Miss Grant to have the pompous parasite Mr. Ramsay with his empty intellectual pretension praised, a man much like Woolf's own father, Leslie Stephen, who preyed on his children and who would have poisoned their future if he had lived long enough to do so. I burned my paper on Lily Briscoe in my wastebasket after my parents had gone to bed. Even now, my stomach turns when I think about it.

Spring came. I continued to thrill to Ivan's rebellion. I thought about the nature of God. I stopped going to church. I wrote a senior honor's paper on the Grand Inquisitor. Miss Grant told me in confidence that she believed I was headed for graduate school. The last day of school came. I cleaned out my locker; I went to parties; I graduated in a white dress. My thoughts were on what was ahead. I decided to major in philosophy. I had already preregistered for a Plato class at Harvard and dipped into *The Republic*. Except for a few formalities at graduation, I did not see Miss Grant again until the Christmas vacation of the next year.

I had been too busy, too taken up with the excitement of new friends and new classes to think much about Miss Grant. I was doing well. My Plato teacher, a well-known classicist, had singled me out and invited me to tea at his house where a small coterie of philosophy students gathered. I was no longer so gaunt, no longer so shy. I applied for a summer fellowship to study philosophy in Scotland. What finally took me back to Miss Grant was the need for a recommendation and a touch of nostalgia to see the old school again.

I wrote a formal little note. I would be visiting the school on such and such a date. Could she write me a letter? I could pick it up in the school office.

That afternoon I took my old walk to school, pleasurably thinking back to the days when I had to carry my cello. The school was quiet. Vacation had not yet started for them, but the students had left for the day. I checked with the office. "Miss Grant would like to see you," the secretary said. I went down the old halls, narrower than I remembered. A teacher I didn't know heard my footsteps and looked out of her door suspiciously. I was now an interloper. I hurried on. I took in the familiar musty smell of the woodwork; I anticipated the aroma of Earl Grey brewing in Miss Grant's electric teapot, water sputtering on the hotplate, the packet of British tea biscuits. I hesitated at her closed door. I knocked.

A voice inside told me to come in. and there she was, Miss Grant, unchanged, eternal, sitting behind her desk.

"Sit down." She said. She turned away from me, got up, walked to the small dormer window of her office. I thought back to her lecture on Virginia Woolf's suicide.

"How dare you. How dare you write to me that way, as if you hardly knew me?" The voice was cold, hard, without expression. "After all that we had together."

Panic. No tears. Nothing like tears this time. My impulse was a child's. I thought frantically back to what I could have done, what milk I had spilled, what chore omitted. But of course, how could there be? I had not seen Miss Grant for almost nine months.

She turned so I could see her face. "After all that we meant to each other, to leave without a word. You never came. You never wrote. And now this."

My face flushed red with embarrassment. I shrank down in my seat.

"I gave you all I had, and it meant nothing. Now you want me for a note like that. As if you don't know me, as if we are strangers. Well, I'll write no recommendation."

She took a step back from the window. "You can go." She said flatly.

I fled. I opened the closed door of her office. I flung myself down the stairs. I ran, heart pounding, and did not stop until I was several blocks from the school, heart pounding. Finally, I stopped. I caught my breath, I couldn't go home. Not yet. I couldn't face anyone, talk to anyone. I sat down on the curb, for once oblivious to appearances. I made myself take deep breaths. I looked around at the suburban houses with their neat lawns, houses that I knew I would never live in, or never live happily in any more than Mrs. Ramsay was happy in her house by the sea. I felt myself crushed between them, between the impossible houses and the unfulfilled expectations of Miss Grant.

In the next few years, I put Miss Grant and what had happened out of my mind. She had treated me shamefully. To speak that way to a student. I vowed that if I ever became a professor, I would never treat anyone that way, never put that sort of burden on a student. And never—not that I was ready yet to put this name to it—never would I fall in love with one of them. At moments, I even allowed myself to think that my paper on Lily Briscoe had not been that bad after all.

But of course she was right. She had been right about the paper, and she had been right about me. I had failed, failed to understand the value of what she taught me, and then failed to understand the cost of teaching it to me. I had not understood the price of thought that goes beyond Mr. Ramsay's superficial *A*-to-*B* logic. I had not understood the passion that drives any real search for truth. Imperfect, cruel, impatient, and intolerant, Miss Grant may have been, but she taught me a lesson that it took a long career as a philosopher to learn, a career more like that of the once-despised Lily Briscoe than of the successful and celebrated Mr. Ramsay. All those difficult years as a fledgling philosopher, prey to the seductions of patronage, tempted to easy academic success, reading *To the Lighthouse* that senior year with Miss Grant went a long way to protect me from the frustrations, the inequities, the humiliations that plague and demoralize a woman philosopher.

10

Philosophy and Life: A Singular Case of Their Interconnection

Ofelia Schutte

In this chapter, I will try to narrate what it has been like for me to be a Cuban-born woman in professional philosophy in the United States during the last three decades of the twentieth century. I will focus on the connection between my life and the paths of my philosophical career, taking into consideration my commitment to do philosophy in close connection with lived experience. I will also dwell on experiences that highlight my participation in philosophy as a Latina feminist. Some of these identifications developed over the course of the years, but they are evident now as I write this chapter. As I wrote, the audience I had in mind were younger women in the profession, former students at all stages of their careers, and people who have read my work but perhaps know little or nothing about my life or about me as a person. For this reason I have highlighted the connections between my life and philosophy, occasionally situating my experience in the context of politics. This narrative is only a beginning of a *testimonio* (or witnessing) regarding the insights my life has allowed me to bring to philosophy, the prejudices I have faced and overcome, and the principles to which I have dedicated my work so that others may benefit in the future.

FROM GRADUATE SCHOOL TO ASSISTANT PROFESSOR

My graduate career in philosophy started out without much of a conflict. I was fortunate to have met with no major gender or ethnic prejudices at the institutions where I took graduate degrees in philosophy. I received an M.A. in philosophy from Miami University of Ohio in 1970. At the time, I started teaching part-time in the area's colleges. Prior to the M.A. in philosophy, I

had earned an M.A. in English, so I had plenty of things to do. In my family, there was no expectation that I should get one master's degree, much less two. Neither was there any expectation that I should go on for a Ph.D. I used to socialize with faculty at the time, because I lived in a small town. The more faculty I met and interacted with, the more I realized that I had the talent and motivation to get a Ph.D., and I spent some time deliberating whether I should go on in English or in philosophy. I decided on philosophy because it seemed that I had a lot of questions that perhaps the study of philosophy might satisfy. When I received a fellowship at Yale's graduate program, I was very happy that I had chosen philosophy—and that, in a way, philosophy had chosen me. I said farewell to Ohio and packed my bags for New Haven, Connecticut, which ultimately became a decisive turn in my life. What followed were five more years of graduate school and, subsequently, twenty-four completed years in the profession (as of 2002). I did not experience being a "woman in philosophy" in a negative sense until I came to Florida. As I recall, students were strongly encouraged at both Miami University and Yale to succeed whatever the gender, at least from an academic standpoint. Unfortunately, this ethos was not to be the case during my lengthy career in philosophy at the University of Florida (1978–1999), where, despite all the wonderful things that took place, I was the recipient of mixed messages regarding my place in the profession.

The best thing that happened to me in the early days of my career was having a very supportive advisor, Professor George Schrader. Although he was a Kant scholar and I wanted to write on Nietzsche, he came to my aid when I was in search of a dissertation advisor. George's guidance led me to stay away from routine approaches to the subject matter and to carve out a path of my own, even if it was uncharted. What would be important in the long run, although I did not perceive its importance immediately, was George's support for feminist scholarship. He encouraged me to criticize Nietzsche from a feminist perspective, if I had reason to do so. His guidance, which years later evolved into a friendship, continued in the first years after I had left Yale.

At the time of my graduate studies at Yale—from 1973 to 1978—there were no feminist courses in graduate school, and only a few female faculty taught in my department. Even though I had some feminist friends, it took a while before I considered myself a feminist. At the time, I thought feminist philosophers were women like Alison Jaggar and Marilyn Frye, both of whom I admired tremendously. They were doing feminism out of the British and North American traditions. Coming from a Latin American background in its understanding of gender and sexual difference, I could see only some of my concerns reflected in their works. In addition, I thought my concerns could fit under the label of humanist, with feminism being a subset of humanism and its concern for human rights. But then I moved to Florida, and my perspective quickly grew in awareness. Specifically, I began to notice that in social relations undertaken as part of my work, I was treated differently from the way my male peers were treated. I began to see that, before anything else, what stood out was my gender and that my sexual difference from the male put me in second place. I recall one of my first social experiences after moving to Florida. The new faculty had been invited to a reception at a faculty member's home. I happened to arrive at the same time as a young man who was also single. We both stood at the front door of our hosts when the hostess came to the door. She spoke directly to him, welcoming him to the university and to the area. Next she looked at me, saying, "And are you his lovely wife?" From that day on, it was a struggle for equality and for equal recognition among many of my peers. I was not in the Northeast; I was in the South, and that difference mattered in 1978. Had things changed by 1998, or by 2002? Perhaps the rest of my chapter will provide some clues.

I began teaching my first undergraduate feminism course a year or two after arriving at the university. I was fortunate that another feminist—Jeffner Allen—had preceded me in the department. When she left physically, one thing that remained was a course on feminism in the undergraduate catalog. I began teaching that class, at first using books by Mary Daly and other feminist stars of the period. Later, as some of the early philosophy anthologies began circulating, I moved from individual books to edited collections. Initially, especially during the period when I was untenured and when everyone else in my department was tenured, my colleagues did not feel threatened at all by my presence. On the contrary, they seemed to enjoy it. At the end of the 1970s, every male colleague who thought he must appear "politically correct" in fact declared himself a feminist. Males who were not feminist were perceived to be from the age of the dinosaurs. (Later, in the 1990s, a conservative turn occurred. A few male colleagues adopted antifeminist philosophical identities explicitly and with a good conscience—for which they were rewarded by an antifeminist department chairman. Whatever they thought of feminism in the public sphere, it was feminism *in philosophy* that they strongly rejected. They assumed their view was both open-minded and liberating to philosophy, just as they banned feminist philosophy from their courses and departmental reading lists.) Retrospectively, I think that all those profeminist political gestures of the 1970s and early 1980s may have vanished in thin air had they been given a proof by fire, which they were not. Instead, in my very earliest tenure-track years, everything was tranquil as far as supporting women was concerned. Everyone supported women, and everyone supported me in particular, a progressively minded Latina feminist. It was a transitory period that would soon come to an end.

The 1980 national election brought Ronald Reagan and conservative forces to power. For its part, the university was intent on improving its national reputation. During my pretenure years, there was a university-wide move toward "higher standards." When I got the first indication that I was going to be required to do far more to obtain tenure than the set of males who had preceded me, my gut reaction was that it was a sexist move to get rid of me. In hindsight, however, I see that it was actually the case that the standards for tenure and promotion had gotten tougher—for everybody. These new standards, however, affected women disproportionately in relation to men given that the change coincided with the years more women were entering the professions at the junior ranks in an effort to balance a predominantly male (and white) academy. In any case, I had been working on my book manuscript all along, long before there was any talk of higher standards. As the time for my tenure and promotion consideration grew near, what I needed was to find a good publisher. It was most fortunate that the University of Chicago decided to publish my book on Nietzsche. This book was no longer my dissertation; I had written most of it from scratch during my early pretenure years at Florida. I had even taken trips to Germany and Switzerland, including Sils Maria, Nietzsche's cherished town in the Alps, as I laid the groundwork for my book manuscript. But the point was that I had been doing this on my own, not because any of my colleagues had prompted me to "publish or perish." This context gave a form of originality to my first book that I will always treasure. Luckily, I learned to write what mattered to me, regardless of whether or not it was the right "career move." In this sense, I have benefited strongly from academic freedom, and I have been faithful to my intellectual commitments both in times of good fortune and of adversity. I consider this trait a kind of strength from within that I was fortunate to nourish over time, a kind of remaining true to one's self that probably has sustained my philosophical work through more than one challenging period (and as my perspective changes over time). I suspect my attraction to and dialogue with Nietzsche's works has served to strengthen this type of inner resolve in matters of conscience.

During the period of stress in the tenure-earning process, I consulted my advisor at Yale from time to time for guidance. He told me to keep writing and not to worry, that some scholarly press would publish my book. That sentiment used to frustrate me, since it was such an indefinite prediction. The day I called him about the news from Chicago, he commented: "It couldn't have happened to a nicer person!" One thought crossed my mind when he said this: "He thinks I'm a very nice person." By contrast, not everyone at my job thought I was so nice. As the political climate turned more conservative, I had to become more outspoken in defending my rights—and justly so, for the day would come when no one else would do it for me.

At the time, my work was getting so much attention nationwide that it was easy to bypass the negativity with which I began to be treated by some around me as my national reputation grew. The other side of the coin of my having had to attain higher standards to get tenure was that I had to outperform other members of the department who had attained tenure in past years. Paradoxically, what made everyone happy (the fact that I got my manuscript published by an excellent press) perhaps made some not so happy. Now I had turned into someone they did not know before—an overachiever, an aspiring "star." I got tenure and was promoted to associate professor with two antithetical caveats: on the one hand, I had to prove that what I had done was outstanding; on the other, I had to apologize for the success of my book publication. I was subject to constant mixed messages—yes, do succeed, but not too much, lest you take away attention from the men around you, who have been here longer than you. Years later, when I had attained the seniority invoked here, I was asked to set my interests aside to provide opportunities for younger faculty who have extraordinary promise ahead of them. As a junior faculty member, I had to defer to the senior faculty, but when I reached the status of senior faculty, I was asked to defer to the younger white males in the department. I was trapped in a gender role from which not even feminism could liberate me. It was the simple belief that, in the domain of the logos, a woman should generally be subordinate to a man—that is, if she wanted to be considered a woman. If she did not mind being treated for all intents and purposes as a man, then I don't think she would have been placed in this disadvantageous position. I knew, however, that no matter how much I tried, I could never feel, act, or think "like a man." Neither could I place myself in neuter. For better or worse, I was a woman, and this embodiment was going to remain a part of my writing and my philosophical work. In other words, it was my "luck," as Claudia Card might say, to be born female.[1] To this ambiguous and at times ill-fated "luck," I added a conscious determination to remain both female and feminist. How did I fare as the next stage of my career went on in philosophy?

AFTER TENURE

As usual, when people get tenure, one looks not just at past projects completed but at future productivity. Once my Nietzsche book was finished, I had to think about what my next major project would be. At the time, I had a distinct sense that I wanted to focus on more contemporary issues than Nietzsche (although I continue to appreciate Nietzsche to a large extent because his thought elicits significant contemporary responses). I wanted to move closer to my existential identity and write books about two features of my identity that contributed to my specific perspectives on the world: one, my Cuban (Caribbean, Hispanic, Latino) birthplace and early upbringing, along with the fact that Spanish is my native language and that Latin America is my original cultural home; and two, the fact that I am a woman. Since I was committed to social- and political-liberation projects, I particularly wanted to write about Latin American and feminist liberation. (I'm stating these objectives in the language of the times. It was still the 1980s.) The Nicaraguan Sandinista revolution was trying to survive the attack from the Right, and all over Central and South America, important political changes were occurring. I felt that there was a crucial need for Latin American philosophy in the United States, given this country's proximity and relation to Latin America. In 1985, I won a Fulbright Senior Research Fellowship to go to Mexico and begin work on my project.

In August, I departed for Mexico City, and by mid-September I had found a comfortable place to live in one of the city's nicest neighborhoods, Coyoacán. I rented the upper story of a house located just a few blocks from the Frida Kahlo Museum and from a tree-filled park (a refuge from the city's smog and pollution). Then, something happened that was totally unforeseen. One morning, shortly after I moved to my new apartment, I woke up to find the bed rocking. In a few seconds, I realized I was caught in an earthquake. The entire house was swinging back and forth with such force that I could not stand up straight without falling. Trying to keep my balance, I ran to the exit door, only to find that the key was jammed and that the door would not unlock. After several tries and more swings back and forth of the entire edifice, I managed to open the door, which led to a balcony. At one end of the balcony, on the side of the building, were the only stairs to get to the ground, but it was too dangerous to try to go down these narrow stairs when the entire building was rocking to and fro. I decided to stay right under the entry door's frame for safety and wait the rest of the earthquake out, although I was so fatigued from the stress that I just lay on the floor next to the door and the balcony wall.

Nearby, birds flew in circles around a tall tree, shrieking loudly. I felt I would die within a few minutes. I made my peace with "nature" despite the perceived violence of the earthquake, and I placed my thoughts on my love for my mother and my dog back home. Fortunately, my life was spared. After a few more seconds, the earthquake ended (it was later designated at the magnitude of 8.1). It would take many months before my life returned to its normal pace. In the transition, I developed a much more compelling view of philosophy's connection to life and culture. Like the city in ruins, my identity underwent a crisis, wondering where I belonged: to what life project, to what country, to what language? On that day and for the next few months of my sabbatical, I would live in Mexico City as a foreigner in a stricken land.

Thousands of people did die that day and in the days that followed, buried under collapsed buildings. By some unofficial estimates, up to ten thousand lives were lost. Hospital wings collapsed, killing hospital staff, nurses, doctors, patients, including mothers and their newborn babies. This tragedy had an overwhelming impact on me. (The closest analogy here is the type of effect September 11, 2001, had on many who had never witnessed sudden massive deaths as buildings collapsed in a highly populated urban environment.) When I looked at how the Mexicans dealt with this natural disaster and massive deaths, I found major differences from the way we deal with disasters and natural tragedies in the United States. Here, a discourse focuses on the quantification of material loss and on finding an explanation for the tragedy, as well as on proposing a plan for preventing future loss. In Mexico, there was an appeal to fate and the nobility of accepting God's will. Emotion and even humor were regular outlets in the aftermath of the event. I also found major differences from the way disasters and natural tragedies are dealt with in Cuba, where I grew up and was raised, and where responses to natural disasters tend to be pragmatically oriented. My awareness of culturally distinct ways of dealing with widespread crises and tragedy eventually made me look at philosophy—its genesis, production, and "universal" acceptance—in a radically different light. It led me to understand that philosophy is very much embedded in cultural values and presuppositions that may appear "universal" to its internal epistemic communities but that are really the product of various historical and cultural locations. The book project I had brought to Mexico fell apart after the earthquake. Instead, I tried to reconstruct what it would be like to look at Latin American social thought historically, from the discourses that constituted the specificities of some of its social and intellectual movements. It took me several more years, as well as many important personal experiences, to complete my book, including a return visit to Cuba to see my childhood and teenage neighborhoods after twenty-six years of absence. I was so engrossed in this book project and in everything it symbolized in my life, including the newly awakened contacts with Cuba and the introduction to other parts of Latin America, that I did not have a great deal of time to attend to all the new circumstances that were transforming the Gainesville philosophy department.

THE ASSOCIATE PROFESSOR YEARS

My years as associate professor (1984–1994) were very rewarding professionally, even though after 1986, the circumstances of the University of Florida (UF) Philosophy Department became quite difficult. In the spring of 1986, while I was on sabbatical and a short time after I had returned from Mexico, the department was placed in receivership with the threat of abolition.[2] During my absence, the department split into at least two opposing sides.[3] Several months later, after a review by a college committee, one of the conditions set for the department's reinstatement referred to faculty members' comportment and collegiality. The other major condition was administrative reform. The constitution of the department was suspended because it was considered too democratic. All power was given, at first, to an external administrator, and eventually, to an externally hired chair. Having grown up in Cuba during the military dictatorship of Fulgencio Batista—when the Cuban people had lost all their constitutional freedoms and when a state of self-censorship haunted teachers lest they lose their jobs—I recalled my early childhood and decried the lack of freedom to which we were subjected when our department fell under receivership. No one believed me, though, because except for those of us who were in receivership, the rest of the university was functioning normally.

During the period of receivership, a systematic curricular reform was instituted, which locked in a much more restricted list of approved courses. Two courses I used to teach perished in the process of "reform": a senior course entitled "Philosophy of the Human Condition" and a graduate course on nineteenth-century philosophy (covering European continental philosophers). Other casualties included courses on Marx and, if I recall correctly, on various other individual philosophers, such as Plato and Aristotle. The entire curriculum was purged. Coinciding with the second Reagan presidency, this curricular reform seemed like a political move to rid the department of any conceivable association with Marxism, among other things. But the reforms were defended on the grounds that the department offered far too many courses and that streamlining was necessary. Indeed, outside reviews of the department indicated that far too many courses were listed and that the curriculum needed some structure and change. In retrospect, it seems to me the excess of courses was a product of the university's changing its calendar from the quarter to the semester system a few years earlier; that is, new courses were being added without thought as to what ought to be deleted. For those unhappy with the status quo, it was a good excuse to hit the department with some very tough medicine for an illness that could perhaps have been cured through a gentler, alternative approach.

One undergraduate course that survived the reform was on existentialism. I held on to that as one of my standard courses. Feminism survived as well, and one course on continental philosophy. By this time, I had introduced a course on Latin American social thought, which also survived the purge. During the rest of my career in philosophy at Florida, I kept teaching one or another version of these undergraduate courses, sometimes in alternate years, along with one graduate seminar each year. Overall, my courses tended to draw many students.

Why did I stay at the University of Florida when the philosophy department faculty lost our freedom of representation and self-governance? I really had faith that the university administration would be fair to me and to the others in the long term. The goal of scholarly excellence, which external reviews mandated, was one I always supported. Moreover, there was a great deal of talk during receivership of balancing the needs of the faculty and searching for a chair who would support diversity and pluralism, although as it turned out we were shortchanged on both goals.[4] No one had a crystal ball at the time to read into the future. My main research focused on my Latin American project. The university's library collection in Latin American studies is one of the best in the United States, so with regard to my project, I was in an excellent location. During these years, I became very involved in the Society for Iberian and Latin American Thought (SILAT) as well as the American Philosophy Association (APA). Through SILAT, I met a group of Latinos and Hispanics in philosophy who were very supportive of my work. As I reached a more senior position, I dedicated a great deal of time to mentoring younger Latinos and Latinas in the profession as well as to helping make our contributions to philosophy more visible at the national level. I served two complete terms in the APA committee on Hispanics/Latinos, first as member and then as chair. I also served on numerous other committees for the APA and on the associate editors' board of the feminist journal *Hypatia*. In addition to those with whom I worked at the national level and to those colleagues in various parts of Latin America who extended invitations and personal support, I had a solid network of colleagues in the profession with whom I could share my views and research. A special acknowledgment goes to members of the Radical Philosophy Association who, in the early 1990s, moved walls of ideology and bureaucracy to facilitate my joining them at some of the group's annual meetings in Cuba. My sense of self was so enriched during the years in which I was working primarily on Latin America that the local difficulties in the philosophy department seemed minor compared to the personal growth I was experiencing as a result of writing about Latin American cultural and political issues. I traveled to many conferences, while back home I developed much collegial support among the Latin American studies faculty.

My affiliation with women's studies at Florida also provided continuing intellectual challenges and supportive feminist friendships. In the 1990s, I was active in developing several interdisciplinary graduate courses in women's studies, cross-listed with philosophy. I served on numerous M.A. and Ph.D. committees, helping women students from across the humanities and social sciences. The philosophy department had moved out of receivership in 1989, but its administrative reinstatement was soon filled with disappointments for me. The department kept growing only in one direction—toward analytic philosophy of mind, philosophy of math and science, and related areas. The graduate program was redesigned to require a highly specialized knowledge of Anglo-American analytic subjects and to eliminate a comparable amount of competence in European continental philosophy, in which I was trained. Shortly after the new graduate program went into effect in the early 1990s, I was told that the department admitted very few students, and with new program requirements in place, there would be no need for me to keep teaching graduate courses, at least on a yearly basis, as I had done in the past. The chair told me my areas of specialization did not bring prestige to the department, which made no sense to me at all. My areas of specialization had always been recognized with honors, including the Fulbright Senior Research Fellowship to Mexico. I was one of the best-known senior scholars in the department. It was unthinkable for me not to teach graduate courses in the foreseeable future. I was then told that if I could enlist students from *outside* the department, I could continue teaching my courses; just do not expect any of *our* graduate students to take them, because their schedules will already be full. The condition to bring other students from outside the department to my courses did not prove to be a significant problem. I realized I was being prevented from "reproducing" my areas of specialization in a younger generation of philosophy graduate students. This situation seemed very unfair to me. But then I saw that my courses often attracted twice as many students as the average number who signed up for the philosophy program—and that they attracted many talented students whose joint presence at the seminars created extremely interesting and challenging learning experiences. It was wonderful to work with these University of Florida students, even if I felt the loss of not teaching those in my own department. My interdisciplinary knowledge was strengthened, as was my ability to teach students from different fields. A good number of students asked me to serve on their dissertation committees, which in turn led not only to more interaction with faculty in related humanities and social science disciplines but to updated knowledge linking feminist and recent European philosophy, as well as Latin American theoretical criticism, to theoretical developments in several fields. This type of intellectual development resulted from and strengthened my philosophy of education, which is inclusive, whereas the philosophy department practiced and preached exclusivity of method and canon. The dominant view was that "continental philosophy" was an empty term because the only acceptable philosophical methodology was analytic, even if the object of study were Nietzsche or Heidegger. It became increasingly contradictory for me to function as a senior member of the department.

To confine students to think and write philosophy using only a single method of analysis and to deprive philosophy students of the ability to read texts in traditions other than that of Anglo-American analytic philosophy is, I think, an intellectual blunder. We are graduating Ph.D.'s in philosophy who are poststructurally illiterate or who are illiterate vis-à-vis French feminism, Latin American postcolonial thought, and many other significant nonanalytic bodies of knowledge. The attitude of those who promote these forms of illiteracy is this: such areas do not represent knowledge for us—that is, knowledge of sufficient philosophical significance. The "for us" itself becomes so narrow that the philosophical community is defined in terms of exclusivity. Worse yet, this exclusivity is defended in the name of universal knowledge, in which case it proceeds to exclude everything outside it with a good conscience. Unwilling to entertain significant differences in the methods and scope of philosophical inquiry, how could they see that there is philosophy outside this circle? Unless those in power who have such a view realize there is a gap in their knowledge that spells ignorance in someone else's mirror, new generations of students may never know what they missed. I believe that sooner or later the façade of rationality as logical control over discourse will break down in many philosophers' lives. When logical analysis breaks down, hermeneutics and other forms of approaching discourse, such as those engaged in by continental philosophers, may still be viable. The definitive experience that made me come to this realization was my mother's illness.

THE FULL PROFESSOR YEARS

My promotion to full professor was uneventful. After the publication of my second scholarly book and a term as a Bunting fellow at the Radcliffe Research Center, my promotion to full rank could no longer be held back. Over the years of my academic studies and career, however, I had romanticized what it would like to be a full professor. Only after I reached this rank did I realize that, at least in my case as a Latina feminist and a specialist in fields that apparently put in question the narrow identity of the department, I had little power or influence over what went on in my home department. I don't think I had any more influence than I had as associate professor. This realization added a great deal of unhappiness to my situation, especially in one case when a younger female colleague asked me for help fighting the practices that placed her in a subordinate position to her junior peers. There was nothing I could do to change the routine operation of the department or the way the chair decided on committee assignments. On big items like the tenure vote, one can draw as many resources as are available in an institution to make sure that each woman gets a fair hearing. But when it comes to daily, routine matters in one's employment where tiny things people do get on one's nerves, we had no institutional procedures in place to promote or support equal treatment. In my case, I fought even small irritating behaviors time and again because I had no special problem being direct and outspoken. But many women feel too vulnerable to speak out, especially if they are untenured and if they work in a department where a certain degree of docility to male authority is expected as part of a person's work assignment.

Although I am Hispanic and although discrimination also occurs against Hispanics (as our ethnic group is legally referred to in the state of Florida), in most of this chapter I have represented my disadvantage vis-à-vis my colleagues in terms of gender rather than ethnicity. If anything, I think my ethnicity may have protected me from further discrimination in some respects. It is so obvious that I am Latina that to deny me equal treatment would appear to many to be racist. To discriminate against Hispanics in the state of Florida is not a smart idea. One of the objects of devaluation I experienced in the philosophy department (by a small minority who controlled policy)[5] was my area of specialization in Latin American philosophy. It could be argued that this treatment meant a simultaneous devaluation of my person as part of a culture that allegedly could not produce a philosophy that counted for anything associated with "prestige," as it was stated from a narrow standpoint. Yet the devaluation of Latin American philosophy I experienced was nothing compared to the devaluation of feminist philosophy and of issues perceived to pertain to women. As a result, my mother's illness eventually provoked a contradiction between the principles by which the philosophy department outlined and defined its values and my feminist ethical principles.

I was fortunate that when my mother's illness intervened in my life, I was already a full professor and had a long solid record of professional achievements. Although her illness was gradual, a few periods of intense crises happened from time to time and disrupted my attention from work, career, and employment. During the entire length of her illness, I had to keep working because work is my only source of income. I also found that working, difficult as it was sometimes, provided a source of strength from which to face and weather some of the existential crises induced by the nature of her condition. My mother was afflicted with a form of dementia that, unlike Alzheimer's, came and went at unpredictable intervals. Sometimes she lost her mind, and at other times, she regained it, with the rhythm between the two being unpredictable and uneven. Her good periods could last months, hours, or minutes. The first time my mother lost her mind temporarily (although I did not know ahead of time it would be temporary), I had to switch out of the view that the thing that gives human beings their dignity is their rationality. I held on to the view of my mother's dignity despite her loss of reason. I tried to analyze every aspect of her disease as much as possible so that I could understand it, but at the same time, I realized that in order to understand her, I had to reach out to her in her state of unreason. This task seemed very difficult to do, for at the time, she seemed to be in another mental universe. I kept talking with her and visiting her at the hospital every day, and after much effort and many painful experiences, her mind came back, at least sufficiently to continue having a meaningful relationship with cognitive features.

None of my philosophy colleagues understood what I went through during this period. In the official view, philosophy was the logical analysis of statements and concepts. Life, existential pain, dementia, or caring for those in desperate need of attention had purportedly nothing to do with philosophy. For me, though, philosophy was of the essence in how I responded to this situation of critical need. My background in phenomenology and my interest in psychoanalysis and the unconscious carried me through this period. When my mother's discourse lost "rational" meaning, I looked for meaning in partial images and sentence fragments. Her speech comprised brief and disintegrating clusters of meaning that could still evoke personality features and a direction for possible action. I felt that the brain held a deep reserve of power well beyond the mechanism of conceptual rationality. When one system failed, perhaps the other, although chaotic and not self-sufficient, could be partially enabled to survive the crisis. The fact that I was able to maintain a close and communicative relationship with my mother throughout the five and a half years she was ill proves to me that the methods of reasoning I had learned in hermeneutics and continental philosophy are far superior in addressing care-oriented relationships of the kind that touched my life. Yet during this period, one of my UF colleagues published a book where he tried to prove that there is no continental philosophy worthy of its name at the end of the twentieth century. What a futile endeavor! Does anyone really believe that a field's contributions to knowledge can be dismissed so easily or that reality can vanish when it becomes inconvenient for people to acknowledge it? I suppose I was also expected to do my colleague the courtesy of disappearing from view, since my very presence as an active and engaged philosopher in the department put in question the adequacy of the conceptual framework on which he relied. It was time for me to expand my horizons and seek a more hospitable environment for my work.

JOINING WOMEN'S STUDIES

In 1999, I had a chance to move to a joint appointment in women's studies and philosophy at the University of South Florida (USF) in Tampa. I was offered the job of chair of the women's studies department. With very mixed feelings about leaving the University of Florida in Gainesville, I took the job in Tampa. I knew I needed a feminist environment to continue to work productively. The situation in Tampa is very different from that of Gainesville. Currently, the USF Philosophy Department is friendly to both analytic and continental philosophy, so all the work I do is considered relevant to its undergraduate and graduate programs. Even though I serve as chair of women's studies, last year the philosophy department changed its governance document so that I could become a full voting member of the department. Graduate students are referred to my courses, and I have worked closely with department faculty on various committees. There is growing interest in reaching Latin American philosophers, and there is significant student interest in feminism. My role in women's studies gives me an opportunity to continue work in interdisciplinary feminist theory and in Latin American feminisms. I do miss the University of Florida, where I worked for twenty-one years and where I undertook the major steps of my career from assistant to associate to full professor. Nevertheless, I feel lucky that I love so many aspects of higher education that I can function well in various university environments. I feel tremendously enriched on a personal level by everything I have done professionally and by the knowledge that I have contributed to so many students' lives in a positive way. Over the course of time, I have also learned from my mistakes and have tried to move toward the future constructively. Recently, I have had very moving experiences regarding the recognition and impact of my work. For example, SPEP (Society for Phenomenology and Existential Philosophy) did a panel on my work,[6] and the College of Arts and Sciences and the Philosophy Department at Miami University of Ohio invited me to deliver a Distinguished Alumni Lecture. New and old friends continually invite me to participate in conferences and events, where I have given and continue to give many lectures. I am writing on new areas of postcolonial feminism that I find very exciting. When I complete my term as chair, I hope to write my next book and return to the life of a full professor—a way of life that still has so much to offer despite this time of budget cuts and economic structural adjustments. Wherever my work takes me, I will be grateful to everyone who has helped to make it possible—teachers, friends, colleagues, students—and to the cultural locations and institutions in the United States and abroad that supported their efforts.

NOTES

1. Claudia Clark, "Gender and Moral Luck," in *Justice and Care: Essential Readings in Feminist Ethics*, ed. Virginia Held (Boulder: Westview, 1995), 79–98.

2. The university received a lot of press coverage on the receivership. According to the Alachua County Library District Catalog (WebCat), from which the following information is transcribed, the *Gainesville Sun* published articles on the following topics: "UF's philosophy department put into receivership, controversy," June 8, 1986, 1a; "[Classics chair] Gareth Schmeling chosen as administrator of UF's philosophy department," June 12, 1986, 5c; "Michael Bayles, UF ethics professor, quits citing poor standards," February 4, 1987, 1b; "UF philosophy department faces another review," February 27, 1987, 1b; "UF cuts funding for the philosophy department," March 12, 1987, 1a; "[UF President] Marshall Criser supports funding cutback for philosophy department," March 19, 1987, 1a; "3 UF professors sue to prevent abolition of philosophy department," March 24, 1987, 1b (see also "3 Philosophy Professors Sue U. of Florida," *The Chronicle of Higher Education,* April 15, 1987, p. 2); "Rally to be held in support of the UF philosophy department," April 7, 1987, 1b; "UF philosophy department protesters march on dean Charles F. Sidman," April 8, 1987, 1b; "Dispute surrounding the UF philosophy department remains unsettled," April 9, 1987, 8b; "UF willing to begin search for philosophy department head," April 14, 1987, 1b; "3 prominent philosophers recommend salvaging UF philosophy department," November 15 1987, 1b; "Committee formed to run UF philosophy department," November 17, 1987, 1b; "UF philosophy department endorses committee idea to govern the department," November 28, 1987, 1b; "UF philosophy department works its way to independence," January 5, 1988, 1b; "UF philosophy department seeks chairman," February 16, 1988, 2b; "UF philosophy department slowly recovering from receivership," October 30, 1990. The press release for the November 28, 1987, story was prepared by myself and Ellen Haring (department chair in the 1970s). The letter to the dean accepting the committee's recommendations, of which I still have a copy, was signed by all members of the department except one who thereafter left the university. The agreement expressed in this letter, which I drafted and for which Ellen and I obtained department consensus (which was not an easy task at the time), marked the important transition to move out of receivership. Despite these actions, I was excluded

from membership in the "Executive Committee" appointed to take charge of the department's future and thereby both denied a vote in the selection of the future chair and excluded from all social activities to which only members of the "Executive Committee" were invited—for example, receptions for national visitors. Even though I was a member of a national APA committee at the time and had reason to get to know a guest, I was expressly denied entry to these socials because I was not a member of the department's "Executive Committee." I appealed the exclusion to the dean's office, which was willing to consider it, but my appeal was rejected by my own peers on the grounds that the committee was already "too large." The committee consisted of several members from outside the department (all male) and four department members, of which only one was a woman. It included no minorities. On another note, Michael Bayles, who left the UF philosophy department in 1987 to take a position at the "rival" Florida State University in Tallahasee, published a related article in the June 1988 issue of *Teaching Philosophy* (11:2, pp. 97–111) entitled "Lessons of Florida," in which he narrates and analyzes his unhappy experiences at UF, primarily from 1985 to 1987. Sadly, three years after leaving UF in August 1990, Bayles, now an FSU philosophy professor, died in Tallahassee, having taken his own life. (An obituary appeared in the August 9, 1990, issue of the *Gainesville Sun*.) Articles on the department's receivership controversy also appeared routinely in the student newspaper, the *Independent Florida Alligator*. Occasional coverage appeared in the *Miami Herald* and the *St. Petersburg Times*. Bayles' article offers documentation on press coverage in Gainesville and elsewhere.

3. Initial issues included newly hired faculty members' concerns about existing academic standards and old-time faculty members' concerns that resources were being diverted primarily to support the newcomers, leaving the rest excluded or marginalized. I was not a player in these events since I was out of the country on sabbatical, but I could not escape being affected by them after I returned. In the course of time, issues of academic freedom and freedom of speech played a prominent role in the debates.

4. Specifically, the "Report of the External Review Committee for the Department of Philosophy at the University of Florida," prepared by Professors Joel Feinberg, Ernest Sosa, and Richard Schacht in the fall of 1987, stated: "The members of the department as presently constituted have various special research interests and competences of useful and legitimate kinds. These specialties in the department give it its own distinctive character, which we are quite prepared to acknowledge as one of its positive features." It went on to say: "But a distinctive character is best cultivated and displayed in a department in which areas of inquiry central to the discipline traditionally and currently are well represented" (p. 5). Unfortunately, in subsequent years, the latter sentence would be taken out of context by persons in power to make sure the "distinctive character" of the department commended here would one day be erased from memory.

5. Several faculty members in the department always had views that were much more collegial and open-minded, but they had little influence over decision making and policy.

6. The papers will appear in a forthcoming issue of *Hypatia*.

11

Autobiography of a Whistle-Blower

Kristin Shrader-Frechette

The story of how I came to philosophy is less about intriguing books than about inspiring people. People with a passion for social justice. People with an insatiable curiosity about science and epistemology. Ultimately they were doers and not merely thinkers. Their example taught me to move from philosophical analysis to philosophical action.

In 1998, I became lead plaintiff in a class-action lawsuit against the University of South Florida (USF) that involved alleged skimming of federal grant funds, false public records, unreported salary payments, salary discrimination, severe retaliation, and my being stalked by convicted felons. Although all the claims in this chapter are my opinions, I believe the independent factual evidence is compelling and invite readers to draw their own conclusions. Until they happened to me, I never would have believed such events were possible in a major state university. The experience taught me that blowing the whistle can be more complex than traditional ethical norms suggest and far more dangerous than the civil- and criminal-justice system can alleviate.

MY MOTHER THE ACTIVIST

What lead me to the 1998 actions? More than anything, my mother. Mildred Shrader made a difference in the world. She lived the belief that some injustice is so wrong it ought never be tolerated. Raised in a rural African American town in Kentucky, she was a leader in Kentucky civil rights causes and active in both the women's movement and the peace movement. She was the first whistle-blower and activist I knew.

As a child, sometimes Mom's outspokenness embarrassed me. I remember wishing she would just stay at home, keep quiet, and continue canning garden vegetables for our family of nine. When friends came to visit, I remember hoping she would not say anything controversial. Not until late adolescence did I fully realize how fortunate we all were to have her. Not until she was dying, six years later, did I realize how profoundly she had shaped me.

Mom had left art school to marry Dad, and our house was usually a noisy, disorganized swell of artists, activists, students, teachers, and children. A skilled portrait and landscape painter who never managed to balance her checkbook, Mom read voraciously. Weekly she would take all seven of us children to get library books, in multiples of ten, so that we could remember to retrieve them all. Every Friday morning, Mom would be shouting: "I only have forty-eight; who has the other two?" Or "There are only thirty-nine; help me look for the other one."

Mom and Dad designed and built a house in Fern Creek, Kentucky, near Newburg, a large African American settlement. As a result, in the late 1950s we grew up on the only racially integrated part of Jefferson County, and some of my sisters and brothers, like Christopher, made their best friends in Newburg. Christopher and his friend Walter ("Bubba," they called each other) spent a good deal of time thinking up ways to get the better of the local racists. They had a deadpan routine that they would use to challenge segregated clubs or neighborhoods. Once Chris went to "join" the local Moose Club, the chief source of entertainment in Fern Creek. After he had paid for a family membership, Chris mentioned that he and his "brother" would stop by to play pool. When they did so, Walter would be the only colored face in a room full of white pickup-truck owners. The ensuing situations, with Christopher and Walter doing their deadpan exchanges, were the subject of many raucous dinnertime stories. Chris and Walter would always "win" such conflicts, at least in the retelling.

By the early 1960s, my mother had become the first white member of the NAACP in the state of Kentucky. A common christening name for newborn girls in Newburg was "Mildred," for their white godmother. When Mom and Dad marched and sang in civil rights protests, they often pulled the two youngest of my brothers and sisters, behind them, in our old, red-metal, "Flyer" wagon. Later she became a leader in Kentucky's open-housing movement. Once her youngest children were in school, Mom went to college. When she was diagnosed with bone cancer, she had been teaching high school English only a year, in the poorest slum of Louisville. Mom had the first environmentally induced cancer that I knew of, caused by repeated X rays. Later I learned that the U.S. Office of Technology Assessment confirmed that up to 90 percent of all cancers are environmentally induced and theoretically preventable.[1] Mom need not have died at age 45. Her death, as well as her life, put a human face on the monumental societal failure to practice environmental ethics and to assess the consequences of technological risks.

AN ACCIDENTAL PHILOSOPHER

Growing up in Fern Creek, Kentucky, made all of us brothers and sisters nature lovers, risk takers, practical jokers, questioners, readers, and hard workers. To go to school and music lessons, we often climbed fences and crossed streams. As children, we spent virtually every daylight moment outdoors, roaming and exploring. Each June, our family loaded our flatbed trailer with Army surplus tents, canteens, tarps, a kerosene cook stove, and our sleeping bags. National parks, all across the United States, were the places where I first questioned how people could believe labor or money somehow gave them property rights to natural resources, things they did not create. Years later, I wrote the first environmental ethics text. It was difficult to get a publisher, because editors said there was no such field. I knew there was. Devastated by my mother's needless death, I knew that environmentally induced cancers were ethical scandals. Exhilarated by wildlands, I knew it was ethically wrong to think of them as mere commodities.

Besides Mom, the Roman Catholic sisters who taught me in high school—the Sisters of Mercy—were the most loving, strong, and intelligent women I had ever seen. They lived what they taught, and they demanded the most of me. At age seventeen, after high school, I distributed my personal treasures and clothing to my brothers and sisters; left my family, the college scholarships, and my boyfriend Steve; and went to live the sisters' vows of poverty, chastity, and obedience. After several days of intelligence and psychological tests the sisters asked me to be a mathematics major at (what is now) Xavier University in Cincinnati. As a senior math major I graduated first in the college class and won a Woodrow Wilson Doctoral Fellowship for which a philosophy professor nominated me without my knowledge. It could be used to study philosophy at any university, and I chose Harvard. But the sisters asked me to attend a Catholic school, so I went to Notre Dame, for a second degree that I had not chosen. Almost by accident, I became a philosopher. But I felt fortunate. Any Ph.D. was a long leap from Fern Creek and more than I ever expected to have.

Getting the Ph.D. was difficult. My mathematics degree had not prepared me for philosophy, and I was ignorant of many of the philosophical classics. There was one other woman in my Ph.D. class of twenty-two, and we became good friends; she was brilliant but dropped out of the program. Discouraged at my ignorance and undeveloped writing, I also might have quit, had it not been for the kindness of fellow student Anita Pampusch and my mentor, Ken Sayre.

A year later, Sayre surprised me when he said I scored the highest in the class on my first four doctoral exams. Then I learned my mother had terminal cancer, and I flunked the fifth and last exam. Mom died a year later. It was difficult to concentrate after her death, but somehow I finished my Ph.D. in four years, in 1972.

Although I loved the sisters, it had become painfully clear that I could not spend my life as a celibate. Leaving the Sisters of Mercy in 1972, I went to teach at the University of Louisville (UL) so as to be near my younger brothers and sisters who were still trying to cope with Mom's death. Two years later, after we took each other's names, I married a brilliant, bearded mathematician, a New Englander, a peace-and-justice activist, a follower of Dorothy Day and the Catholic Worker. Mom would have been glad to know that, as a student, Maurice had marched on Washington. He stood in the crowd to hear the Martin Luther King speech, "I Have a Dream." As our children were born, in 1977 and 1980, Maurice and I juggled our teaching and activism schedules so that one of us was usually with them. Their childhood was a magnificent, but sleep-deprived, time for us. It also was a professionally difficult time because, before tenure, I naïvely had tried to stop use of faulty scientific methods in an Environmental Protection Agency (EPA) document that would have helped some powerful vested interests. The delight of bringing our first child, Eric, home from the hospital was shattered by reporters hounding me about the EPA study. At the happiest time of my life, suddenly my career seemed over, and tenure looked impossible. I thought the vested interests would destroy me. A UL physicist and vice-president, John Dillon, proved me mistaken and taught me it was not wrong to be afraid, only wrong to let my fear stop me from acting.

WORKING FOR JUSTICE

My Louisville years involved not only teaching and research in theoretical philosophy of science and ethics but also practical work on civil rights and desegregation, work with the ACLU, Appalachian coal miners, and women's groups. In the mid-1970s, during busing to achieve racial integration, University of Louisville ACLU faculty organized to line the sidewalks of local grammar and high schools. When the students came up the walks, our human wall deflected the food, bottles, and rocks pelted at them.

During the most violent days of busing protests, Pete Seeger came to Kentucky to help us and shared a story that I often tell my own students: During the worst part of the Vietnam War, Seeger was walking late on Christmas Eve in Times Square. The icy square was virtually deserted, except for a young man—a Quaker—carrying a sign reading "Stop the War." Seeger stopped the fellow and asked, "Do you really think, by carrying that sign on this deserted square, that you are going to change the world?" "I don't know," the Quaker said, "but I'm hoping, if I carry this sign, at least the world won't change me." I remember hoping the world wouldn't change what Mom and the sisters gave me.

Even in the 1970s, Kentucky was in many ways an untamed place. Many of the mountain papers had been bought or bribed by coal interests. The few that had not, like the *Mountain Eagle*, had mysterious fires. Each time "the Eagle" burned, the editor would come to Louisville, and another faculty member and I would arrange a bluegrass benefit concert to buy a new printing press and get him back in business. The caption on my favorite concert poster was the same as the Eagle's bannerhead: "It still screams." It still screams about justice for coal miners and Appalachians.

ENVIRONMENTAL JUSTICE

In the late 1970s, after townspeople from Morehead, Kentucky, asked for help in investigating a local radioactive waste facility, Maxey Flats, I turned some of my philosophy of physics research to more practical matters, like the methods used to calculate the probability of a nuclear accident or the modeling assumptions used to predict migration rates of radioactive leachate. Soon I learned that vested interests almost always used flawed scientific methods to justify siting a dangerous facility in some region where residents were politically or economically powerless to stop it. Funding from the National Science Foundation (NSF) gave me a three-year postdoc in hydrogeology; then another, in economics; and later, one in population biology. These gave me the ability to investigate both theoretical problems in philosophy of science as well as scientific and ethical problems related to environmental injustice. Environmental injustice occurs when vulnerable people—such as African Americans, Latinos, Native Americans, or Appalachians—bear disproportionate burdens of environmental pollution and resource depletion, simply because they are not powerful enough to fight vested interests.

Despite my passion for it, this early work with environmental justice was something of a professional oddity. In the late 1970s, most philosophers neither did such practical research nor worked on NSF grants with practicing scientists.

At Maxey Flats and in later research, I used a simple strategy that anyone could duplicate. *First*, examine the mathematical and scientific methods used in official risk assessments for a site like Maxey Flats. *Second*, determine whether the studies could have used better scientific/mathematical methods or models. If so, *third*, try to use those methods or models. *Fourth*, check for changed ethical and policy assumptions and consequences associated with the improved methodology. *Fifth*, use these findings and ethical theory to argue for protection of the people likely to be victimized by the flawed assessments. Using these steps, undergraduate and graduate students and I churned out scores of articles, books, and federal research grants.

With delight, I watched the students' efforts often christen them into lifelong public citizenship. Frequently our projects also helped change both policy and public opinion. We worked with Kentuckians to avoid the Marble

Hill commercial reactor; with Latinos to investigate the world's first high-level nuclear dump; with Mescalero Apaches to halt a nearby hazardous waste facility; with Africans to reject hazardous waste shipped to them by developed nations; and with World Health Organization officials debating whether to use the same environmental standards in developed and developing countries. Later, we helped achieve the first major U.S. environmental-justice victory: stopping the unwanted siting of a multinational uranium enrichment facility in a poor, African American, Louisiana community.[2]

INJUSTICE CLOSER TO HOME

Although the environmental-justice work had brought threats from vested interests when my analyses challenged their profits, nothing prepared me for the injustice at the University of South Florida (USF). In 1987, after professorships at the Universities of Louisville, California, and Florida, USF recruited me as its first female Distinguished Research Professor.[3] In part because my husband wanted to take a computer-science job nearby, I accepted the USF offer. Eleven years later, retaliation for my whistle-blowing—about illegal grant skimming, false public records, unreported salary payments, and salary discrimination—forced me to leave the university.[4]

When I came to USF in 1987, Dean Jim Strange said I was the highest-paid faculty member in the college. When I blew the whistle and then was forced to leave the university in 1998—despite fourteen books, outstanding annual evaluations, continuous NSF research funding, and more doctoral students than anyone in the department—my salary had dropped to 70 percent of my peers'. When I left, no females were among the forty-six highest-paid faculty in all (nonmedical) units of the university (the Colleges of Architecture, Arts and Sciences, Business Administration, Education, Engineering, Fine Arts, Nursing, and Public Health). I was still the only female Distinguished Research Professor in all these colleges. Of the four highest-paid female faculty in these colleges, three of us left USF in 1998. What happened?

Part of the answer is that state politicians captured a large educational institution that should be independent of politics. In the early 1990s, over the objections of the USF faculty, the politically appointed Florida Board of Regents named a career Florida politician, Betty Castor, as president of USF. She lacked a Ph.D., research skills, scholarly publications, university-teaching experience, and failed to meet the published job criteria. Yet her handlers touted her appointment as a victory for women's rights. After her arrival, people like Professor A,[5] who had barely achieved tenure, were given deanships and placed in policy positions, and faculty like Professors B and C (see note 3), without doctorates, became USF associate provosts. Given such qualifications, the rest of the USF story was predictable. Trouble began in 1991.

WHISTLE-BLOWING IN 1991: USF GRANT LEDGERS AND THE RETALIATION PROBLEM

In 1991 my grant ledgers showed that USF appeared to be skimming funds from the direct costs of NSF research grants. Even though these illegal deductions were small, I learned that USF had done the same on others' grants. A deduction of a fraction of a percent, given more than $100 million in USF's annual external-research monies, could amount to a large sum. After a year of repeated private requests to stop the deductions, nothing happened. Finally I said I would report USF to NSF unless the deductions ended. They stopped immediately. Later, when I asked a USF vice president if USF had stopped these deductions on all research grants, not just mine, he responded: "That's none of your business."

By attempting to correct the grant-ledger problem internally instead of "going public," I was following one of the classical ethical norms for whistle-blowing: behaving as a loyal employee and allowing employers the chance to correct the problem privately.[6] It was naïve, however, to believe that going through channels would protect me from USF retaliation. Because employees typically are politically and economically more vulnerable than employers, when whistle-blowers privately alert employers to a problem and allow time for it to be corrected internally, employers can engage in both cover-up and preemptive retaliation. A better option might be for whistle-blowers to anonymously reveal a problem to employers, wait for them to correct it, but report it to the federal (or state equivalent) inspector general, again anonymously, if the problem is not corrected within a reasonable time. After raising the problem of grant skimming in 1991, I never again received a substantial salary increase at USF, despite the fact that my annual evaluations were always the highest possible (outstanding). The provost, Tom Tighe, repeatedly overruled the department chair or college dean when they sought to give me significant salary increases.

HELPING A VICTIM OF DISCRIMINATION IN 1993 AND DISCOVERING SALARY INEQUITIES

In 1993, one year after USF corrected the grant-skimming problem, microbiologist Joan Rose phoned me for help. Although Rose had the highest teaching evaluations, the most grants and publications, and although she advised the most graduate students in her department, Rose's department and college (Public Health) voted against her for tenure but, the same year, voted tenure for two lesser-qualified men in the same department. Working together, Rose and I secured the support of senior administrators and researchers, and we were able to reverse her tenure decision. Three years later, however, despite top evaluations, publications, and grants, Rose's salary had fallen below average for her rank and department.

Soon I learned that Rose's story was common at USF. Marine scientist Pamela Muller, at least as well qualified as her male counterpart hired the same year, was paid $16,000 less. Carolyn Lavely, who ran an institute for at-risk children, published widely, and garnered more than $50 million annually in outside grant funding—more than any other USF researcher. Yet her salary was lower than that of less-accomplished men in the same college, some of whom had no grants at all. University officials told Sara Mandell, in Religious Studies, that despite her seniority and accomplishments, her salary was $20,000 below that of average males of her rank and department, "because you have a rich husband." In 1996, when the USF president invited faculty to request salary-equity studies, I did so. As a result of the study, my department chair confirmed my inequitable salary, but Provost Tom Tighe justified the discrepancy by claiming that higher salary increases for comparable and less-qualified males were not part of "normal" pay raises and thus not subject to equity constraints.

The experiences of Rose, Muller, Lavely, and I were typical. USF public records revealed evidence of striking disparities between males and females generally. In the departments of Marine Sciences, Religious Studies, and Psychology, for example, female full professors made an average of $.70, $.70, and $.80, respectively, for every dollar that the average male in the same rank and department made.

1997–1998 Public-Record Salaries of USF Full Professors, Selected Departments

Department	*Average Male Full Professor*	*Average Female Full Professor*
Marine Sciences	$80,097	$56,277
Psychology	$78,710	$62,703
Religious Studies	$74,143	$51,995
Endowed Chairs and Distinguished Research Professors, All Colleges	$104,506	$88,279

Source: Central Florida Regional Database, CFRCICS, USF mainframe computer.

THE 1997 PEP SALARY INCREASES AND PUBLIC-RECORD REQUESTS

In 1996 USF Provost Tom Tighe implemented a Professorial Excellence Program (PEP) to correct salary inequities and award the most senior and distinguished faculty a 10 percent salary increase; however, PEP became another vehicle for USF discrimination and retaliation. In the College of Arts and Sciences, only 25 percent of the female full professors who qualified for the PEP increase received it from Provost Tighe, whereas 69 percent of the male full professors who qualified for PEP received it. The chair of the college PEP evaluation committee, Professor D,[7] said that at least half of the college males, who received the PEP salary increase from the provost, had lower committee evaluations than some female faculty, like myself, who qualified for the award but did not receive it. Such discrimination was consistent with what I discovered in a 1997 article in *Nature*. Using multiple-regression analyses that control for experience and productivity, the authors concluded that a female scientist needs to be approximately 70 percent better (as measured by publications, research grants, and so on) than a male scientist, in the same field, to be evaluated the same as he.[8] Another study showed that female Ph.D.'s fare better in nonuniversity positions in terms of senior-level salaries and advancement.[9]

To understand the USF rationale for paying male and female faculty differently, as in the PEP increases, for nine months (March–December 1997) I made weekly written public-records requests for the same USF salary-equity studies and PEP documentation. Although USF was obliged by law (Florida Statutes 119, 286) to answer promptly the public-record requests, as of May 2000, the university has never given me the salary-equity studies. Instead, it retaliated in three ways. *First*, USF tried to illegally demote me. Without my knowledge, USF changed my job classification and title on the USF mainframe computer: In 1987 I was hired as a "Distinguished Research Professor," salary classification code 9006; yet in 1997 USF tried to change my title and job to "Distinguished Service Professor," code 9007. The salary range for the correct 9006 position was approximately $25,000 higher than for the position to which USF tried to demote me. Amazingly, Professor F (in the USF School of Nursing) said that, several years earlier, USF had successfully changed the job-classification codes of all the female nurses after they requested salary-equity studies. After illegally demoting the nurses, USF argued that they were not underpaid, relative to their (changed) job-classification codes. *Second*, USF also retaliated, despite a staff of at least nine in-house attorneys, by hiring an expensive external attorney, Thomas Gonzalez, at taxpayers' expense, to respond to my public-records requests. Gonzalez had made headlines five years earlier after his firm admitted selecting people to do "surveillance" on whistle-blowing faculty who sued USF for retaliation (see note 13). *Third*, when *Tampa Tribune* Reporter E made the same public-records request as I, USF gave the salary-equity study to the reporter within a week, but neither USF nor Gonzalez has given it to me, contrary to Florida law, after more than three years. Associate Provost Phil Smith repeatedly lied when he said there were no such USF documents. Such retaliation suggested why, in the four years immediately prior to the appointment of

President Castor, only four federal lawsuits were filed against the university, but in the subsequent four years, there were seventeen.[10] From 1989 through 1998, federal lawsuits against USF increased by 425 percent, even though the student-body size remained roughly the same, and the faculty grew by only 12 percent.

USF's illegal refusal to supply public records, its subsequent harassment and intimidation through an outside attorney, and its attempting to demote me after it had touted me for years as one of its "star" faculty members was puzzling. In violating public-records laws, what was USF trying to hide?

DISCOVERING SECRET SALARY PAYMENTS AND MULTIPLE BOOKS IN 1997–1998

Evidence showed that USF had three crucial things to hide: illegal discrepancies in salary payments; illegal "surveillance" on whistleblowing faculty (that it admitted under oath in an earlier whistle-blower trial); and salary inequities that were larger than it claimed.

When USF did not promptly answer my public-records request for salary data and equity studies, I used my password (available to USF federal grant recipients) to examine coded payroll records on the USF mainframe computer. It showed a number of faculty were paid on multiple accounts, and some of these payments exceeded the salaries listed on the legally binding USF public records. After downloading date-stamped computer evidence of the discrepancies, I placed it in a safety-deposit box.

During the summer and fall of 1997, I repeatedly met with USF President Betty Castor, Provost Tom Tighe, and several associate provosts, especially Phil Smith. Telling them about the salary discrepancies and inequities, I promised to remain quiet if they corrected the situation. Within two months after I spoke privately to them, my department chair was removed, and another philosopher was appointed to replace him, even though the new chair retained his full-time position on another campus, an hour away. One of his first acts as chair was to move my office, overnight, without my knowledge, and to dump all my books, records, and personal materials, in disarray, in another office (the same size) only four feet away from the original office. Although I was the senior faculty female by rank at USF, suddenly my secretarial support was withdrawn, my grant reimbursements were lost or delayed, I was without a computer for five months, and my graduate students were not paid for months. Interestingly, this newly appointed chair was one of those who received extra salary dollars not reported in USF public records, as required by law (see section 11). I was playing by the rules, working within normal channels to try to correct a problem, but the university was not.

During seventeen months of constant harassment and retaliation, the university did nothing to correct the salary books and inequities, although the president repeatedly promised me, "I'll take care of it." In December 1997, after remaining silent for six months and alerting officials to the problems, I wrote the president a final letter which I had date-stamped by her office. In it I asked her to correct the situation so that I would not be forced to blow the whistle.

THE 1998 LAWSUIT AND STALKING BY TWO CONVICTED FELONS

Because USF did nothing to correct the salary books and inequities, several faculty members hired attorney David Linesch to take the case on contingency as a class-action suit. Linesch said that because the problem of multiple salary books was more difficult to prove than salary discrimination, the case should focus on gender discrimination and introduce the multiple-books and retaliation problems as part of the discrimination issue. Linesch chose Professors Kimmel, Lavely, Mandell, Muller, Rose, and me as plaintiffs for the class of female full professors. They voted for me to be lead plaintiff. Linesch filed suit on February 2, 1998.

Within a week after the suit was filed, three different men began stalking me, blocking my driveway egress, cutting me off, and prowling at night outside our bedroom window. During conversations, our home phone began clicking and making extreme volume changes. Repeated telephone-service records documented a "minor short" on the line. An independent telephone-software expert confirmed that the line was tapped. Even though our family daily received a great volume of mail, often our mailbox would be empty, after the letter carrier said he had placed mail in it. We filed a postal report because of our mail problems. After several weeks, I was able to give auto tag numbers and descriptions of some of my stalkers to the police, so they could question suspects. Later, I identified two of the stalkers, convicted felons Galen Jelskey and Felon Y (see note 5), from a police photo pack. Jelskey served time for assault and battery on women and on police officers, and Felon Y had four grand-theft convictions, some for stealing weapons. Both were on parole when they stalked me. The police identified Jelskey and charged him with criminal (felony) stalking. The third stalker was USF Undercover Policeman Z (see note 5). Because Felon Y and Z had followed me for months but had not cut me off or overtly threatened me, as Jelskey had, the police said that they could not charge anyone but Jelskey.[11]

Yet, under oath, USF and its attorneys, including Gonzalez, denied engaging in "surveillance" of me. Nevertheless, according to written confirmation of Carol Spiegel (wife of USF whistle-blower and orthopedic surgeon Phil Spiegel, who won a million-dollar judgment against USF), Jelskey was "almost certainly" the same man who stalked her six years earlier. When one of the USF lawyers admitted, under oath in the Spiegel case, that the university had done "surveillance" of whistle-blower Spiegel and his wife, the admission hit the front pages of Florida newspapers. The *Tampa Tribune* said that attorney Gonzalez had selected the "investigators" doing the "surveillance,"[12] and the USF attorney who admitted the "surveillance" was promptly fired. Why were convicted felons stalking the wife of whistle-blower Spiegel while he was away at work?

In addition to Carol Spiegel's corroboration of Jelskey's tie to USF, graduate student Peter Shea also witnessed a stalker with USF-related auto tags at our home. He signed an affidavit for the police. Fellow plaintiff Sara Mandell, president of the USF faculty union, likewise was followed by a car whose tag appeared to be the same as Jelskey's. Other faculty members who were subject to USF stalking or "surveillance" include Professors G, H, and I (see note 6). After Professor G refused to lie for a USF administrator who wanted him to fire an innocent person, the administrator said he would "get" G, and the "surveillance" began. Professor H, whose spouse had been a faculty union president, experienced telephone surveillance at home when doing USF faculty-grievance work. Professor I had his office repeatedly broken into, at night, and an FBI informant said that USF Undercover Policeman J (see note 3) had done the "surveillance" on him. USF Undercover Policeman J was also the person identified by USF Official K (see note 3) as the person arrested on campus for attempting to enter a faculty office building at night. Likewise, retired USF Police Officer L (see note 6) confirmed that his superiors told him not to arrest USF Undercover Policemen M and N (see note 6), in case they were caught on campus "someplace where they shouldn't be."

USF ATTEMPTS TO COVER UP ITS MULTIPLE BOOKS

Five weeks after stalkers began following and threatening me, on March 13, 1998 USF issued a third set of salary data, in addition to the (secret) computer and public-record data. These new figures confirmed exactly what the lawsuit claimed: there were discrepancies between what USF claimed to be paying people and what it actually paid them.

1997–1998 USF Payroll Data

Sample Faculty Member	*1997–1998 USF Public Records*	*1997–1998 USF Mainframe Payroll Data, 2-2-98*	*1997–1998 USF IRP Report, 3-13-98*
Arsenault	$59,369	$59,369	$71,400
Fellows	$92,140	$102,180	$109,310
French	$119,038	$129,611	$129,611
Hevner	$91,844	$131,206	$131,206
J. L. Smith	$90,003	$97,884	$97,884
Wieand	$70,990	$76,119	$93,055

Through a tip from *Tampa Tribune* Reporter E, I discovered that there was a fourth set of books, one maintained by the Florida state comptroller at the capital in Tallahassee. Evidence showed that USF actually paid some of its administrators more than it admitted in public records.

USF Administrator	*1997–1998 USF Public Records*	*State Comptroller, Phone Verbal Report, 2-23-98*
USF President Betty Castor	$190,892	$210,775
USF Provost Tom Tighe	$169,958	$183,672

USF attempted to cover up its paying some faculty more money than reported in the public records not only by issuing the new salary report on March 13, 1998 but also by three other methods. *First*, the USF president and provost lied in their press release about salaries. *Second*, the state comptroller stopped reporting salaries to citizens, since that was the way I learned about the additional money President Castor and Provost Tighe received. *Third*, USF raised the president's salary the next year, 1998–1999, by the large amount necessary to make her public-record salary consistent with the state-comptroller data. The first method of cover-up, the lies, were most blatant and disturbing because each lie was contradicted by written public records. For example, ten days after Linesch filed the class-action lawsuit, USF President Betty Castor and Provost Tom Tighe called a press conference (on February 12, 1998) and distributed a press release that selectively misrepresented the salaries of approximately forty top USF faculty members. Among its many falsehoods, the press release listed my job title incorrectly, listed me as having a lesser position, and gave my job classification according to the lower-paid 9007 salary code (mentioned earlier), rather than the correct, higher-paid code of 9006. The press release also lied in saying that my salary was "the highest in the department": public records showed that a less-qualified male made $30,000 more per year. The USF lies would have gone unchallenged had not the *St. Petersburg Times* Reporter O faxed me the press release.

HOW THE MULTIPLE SALARY BOOKS MAY COVER UP USF SALARY DISCRIMINATION

The multiple salary books at USF and the resultant cover-up are significant for at least two reasons. *First*, because all USF discrimination or equity investigations/suits employ the false public-record data in their assessments, their conclusions likely underestimate USF discrimination. *Second*, if one uses the secret computer data to calculate USF salaries, then the gap between male and female average salaries appears larger than what USF reports to national professional agencies. USF claimed male professors were paid on an average $5,913 more than female professors for 1997–1998. In reality, the secret computer data suggest the difference is not $5,913 but $8,362, and USF may underreport its gender gap to national authorities.[13]

If AAUP (American Association of University Professors) data are correct, and if the 1997–1998 USF gender gap for full professors was $8,362, then it is more than double the reported AAUP gender gap of $3,638 at U.S. institutions that the courts forced to work toward gender equity.[14] Once one controls for effects of experience and department, nationwide professorial salary data suggest that the average salary deficit for female university professors is 6.6 percent.[15] According to the analysis of Pamela Hallock Muller, the uncorrected USF salary difference for female full professors is 13 percent or approximately double the national average.[16]

USF STALKERS STOPPED IN AUGUST 1999

When large state institutions like USF can use their political power and almost-unlimited taxpayer money for corrupt purposes—to illegally attempt to demote whistle-blowers, to tell PR lies, to hire expensive attorneys so as to thwart public-records laws, to conduct "surveillance" on whistle-blowing faculty, and to employ retaliation—the deck is stacked against justice. In spring 1998, when the stalking continued, I was forced to leave the university, my home, and my family in order to escape severe stress and retaliation. As a consequence, I am now O'Neill Professor of Philosophy and Concurrent Professor of Biological Sciences at the University of Notre Dame. My husband and I commute between Florida and Notre Dame.

In fall 1998, attorney Linesch urged the USF plaintiffs to settle the case. The other five women—none of whom endured retaliation and stalking—settled. They subsequently received substantial base-salary increases (some as much as 40 percent) and annual stipends, as well as lump-sum monies from the $144,000 settlement. The settlement also promised that USF would alleviate the gender discrimination faced by the approximately sixty other USF female full professors in the entire class. To date, nothing has been done for these other women. Attorney Linesch urged me to drop the stalking and retaliation charges, on grounds that they were irrelevant to the case, despite the fact that he had included the retaliation in the original complaint. Worried that USF would continue to stalk and intimidate other whistle-blowers if I settled, I hired another attorney, Steve Wenzel, to stop the stalking and the civil-liberties violations. One of the most devastating aspects of this case, I believe, was attorney David Linesch's using my stalking evidence as a bargaining chip with the university, and then trying to force me to ignore the stalking and retaliation charges. Several of the plaintiffs are not happy with Linesch's behavior.

Despite Linesch, many law-enforcement officers (who requested anonymity) helped me pursue justice: a Temple Terrace police detective who filed criminal (felony) stalking charges against Jelskey, many Temple Terrace police who repeatedly responded to stalking calls and did their best to protect our family, half of my department colleagues who braved retaliation by urging the administration to try to keep me at USF, the state legislator who took copies of the four sets of books to the governor and state prosecutor, the special agent of the Florida Department of Law Enforcement (FDLE) who is investigating USF's civil and criminal violations, and the two Tampa Federal Bureau of Investigation (FBI) agents who spent months trying to follow the trial of skimmed federal grant funds at USF. One FBI agent, in particular, finally stopped the stalkers, in August 1999, after a year and a half of attempted intimidation.

SPRING 2000: TWO KEY WITNESSES

Two key witnesses are able to tie the stalkers to USF. One is Carol Spiegel, wife of USF whistle-blower Phil Spiegel, who wrote that the man who stalked her in 1992–1994 was "almost certainly" Jelskey. The other is graduate student Peter Shea, who saw a car traced to USF undercover policeman Ramirez stalking me. Carol Spiegel died three days after Christmas 1999. Did USF's admitted "surveillance" contribute to her cancer?

In January 2000, Shea underwent his third surgery for melanoma. If Shea testifies in my case, it is our opinion that USF attorney Thomas Gonzalez will use the same bullying and character assassination against Shea in deposition and in trial as he attempted with me. Without Shea, attorney Wenzel says I have "no case," no independent proof that ties USF to my stalkers. Yet Shea's family wants him not to testify, not to leave himself vulnerable to what USF and its attorneys would do to him. Instead they want him to fight his cancer. Without his testimony, I have no choice except to settle the case without trial.

CLOSURE

What has come of the attempt to force USF to obey laws about public records, criminal stalking, salary discrimination, and retaliation against whistle-blowers? The results are mixed.

On the one hand, the whistle-blowers won several victories. Five of the plaintiffs now have additional compensation that, over their lifetimes will likely reach a million dollars. The FDLE is working on civil and criminal charges against USF. The USF president has been forced to resign, and the provost has been replaced. In spring 2000, the state of Florida hired a new USF president, a woman who is a distinguished university scholar. The Temple Terrace Police Department filed criminal (felony) charges against one of my stalkers, and in August 1999, the FBI was able to stop the stalking.

On the other hand, the business of the whistle-blowers is unfinished. Three of the four highest-paid female (nonmedical) faculty, including me, were forced to leave the university. Despite police charges against Galen Jelskey, State Prosecutor Harry Lee Coe did not bring him to trial. (Under investigation by the FDLE, Coe committed suicide on July 12, 2000.) Despite a state official's promise of a grand-jury investigation of USF, it has not yet come. Carol Spiegel, also believed to have been staked by Jelskey, is dead. Peter Shea, the one remaining witness tying my stalkers to USF, is battling cancer, and there is no criminal case without him. Thus, despite all the evidence against USF, I will have to settle the case and hope that the FDLE and the FBI can achieve justice. A church group at USF will receive the settlement monies.

What has the USF ordeal taught me? Despite the partial successes of the USF case, it reveals ethical problems both with the norms governing whistle-blowing, such as trying first to solve problems internally, and with the harms that come to whistle-blowers who underestimate, as I did, the capacity for evil of those they accuse. The case also suggests that whistle-blowers should recognize, ahead of time, as I did not, how difficult it is to obtain justice when one "plays fair" against those who do not, those who have access to virtually unlimited political power, to the media, and to deep taxpayer pockets. Most importantly, the case taught me that bearing the stalking and retaliation would have been impossible without the support of the other USF women.

In environmental-justice work, I learned that correcting wrongs usually is possible only when people work together for a common cause. Fighting the USF injustices has been difficult because there are few such bonds among professors. Academics often are loners, not joiners. The USF women in the class-action suit were an exception. Many current and former USF professors, with knowledge of grant skimming, financial irregularities, stalking, or surveillance, refused even to talk with FBI agents. They did not want to become involved. Our profession seems to ask more of us than this. So does democracy.

NOTES

Final version of manuscript accepted and received July 19, 2000.

1. J. C. Lashoff et al., *Assessment of Technologies for Determining Cancer Risks*, Washington, D.C., U.S. Office of Technology Assessment, 1981, pp. 3, 6ff.

2. See, for example, Daniel Wigley and Kristin Shrader-Frechette, "Environmental Justice: A Louisiana Case Study," *Journal of Agricultural and Environmental Ethics* 8, no. 3 (April 1996): 61–82; and "Environmental Racism and Biased Methods of Risk Assessment," *Risk* 7 (winter 1996): 55-88.

3. The original title for this position was "Graduate Research Professor." The university later changed the title to "Distinguished Research Professor."

4. Copies of original documents (such as USF press releases containing false data, faculty contracts, downloaded salary pages from the USF mainframe computer, public records of reported USF salaries, USF salary-equity studies, date-stamped public-record requests to USF from the author, photos and videotapes of stalkers and the cars, correspondence, faxes, and so on) to corroborate all these charges are located in the author's safety-deposit box at Terrace Bank, Temple Terrace, Florida.

5. My attorney advised me to delete various names throughout this chapter.

6. See, for example, Marlene Winfield, "Whistleblowers as Corporate Safety Nets," in Gerald Vinten, ed., *Whistleblowing* (New York: St. Martin's Press, 1994), p. 29 of pp. 21–32; M. V. Heacock and G. W. McGee, "Whistleblowing," *Business and Professional Ethics Journal* 6, no. 4 (1989): 35–46.

7. My attorney advised me to delete the name here, lest the person become the victim of USF retaliation for revealing this information.

8. Wenneras and Wold, pp. 341–43.

9. S. F. Zevin and K. D. Seitter, "Results of the Survey of Society Membership," *Bulletin of the American Meteorological Society* 75 (1994): 473–90; Julie Winkler, Donna Tucker, and Anne Smith, "Salaries and Advancement of Women Faculty in Atmospheric Science," *Bulletin of the American Meteorological Society* 77, no. 3 (March 1996): 473–90.

10. The lawsuit data are from Clerk of the Federal Court, Middle District of Florida, (computerized) Case Docket Information, 801 N. Florida Avenue, Tampa, FL 33602.

11. Temple Terrace Police Department, Case 98–1783; Information Report 99–03043, Temple Terrace, FL 33617.

12. "USF Spied on Demoted Department Chairman," *Tampa Tribune*, May 15, 1992, front page. See also "Spied Upon Doctor Dreads USF Decline," *Tampa Tribune*, June 2, 1992, Florida Metro, p. 4; and "USF Settles with Former Chairman," *Tampa Tribune*, July 2, 1994.

13. This reported gap appears in part A of report 041637, and USF reported it to the AAUP journal *Academe* (March 1998 issue). It is based on the USF-reported male salary average of $70,356 and the USF-reported female salary average of $64,443. For USF mainframe-computer salaries, see note 7.

14. Office of Institutional Research, Oregon State System of Higher Education, *The Status of Women Faculty*, Salem, Oregon, State Board of Higher Education, June 1997, available at http://www/osl.edu/irs/statwomn.

15. Marcia Bellas, "Faculty Salaries: Still a Cost of Being Female?" *Social Science Quarterly* 74, no. 1 (March 1993): 62–75.

16. See USF IPEDS Faculty Salary Sex Differences Database, "Per Capita Faculty Salaries by Rank and Sex," at http://tikkun.ed.asu.edu/cgi-bin/ntlf2.pl. For Muller's analysis of covariance, see P. Hallock Muller, "Statistical Evidence for the Glass Ceiling for Academic Women at the University of South Florida," unpublished manuscript available from Muller at Department of Marine Sciences, University of South Florida, St. Petersburg, FL 33701.

12

Getting Here from There

Karen J. Warren

I have a bumper sticker taped to the outside of my office door that begins, "Hard work got me where I am today." With intervening artwork—clouds set against a pale blue background—the text then reads, "Where am I?" Each day when I come to my office, I see that bumper sticker. I usually chuckle: hard work surely is part of what got me to where I am today, personally and professionally; it's just that I am not always clear about where that is.

Over the years, when I have described to others some of the challenges I have faced as a woman pursuing a Ph.D. in philosophy during the 1970s, I have often been told, "You ought to write a book about it!" This is not that book, but what I say here provides a glimpse of the sorts of academic experiences that have shaped me as a person and philosopher.

My first formal introduction to philosophy occurred in 1965, in an entry-level philosophy course during my first semester at a university far away from home. The philosophy professor, a truck driver in his first career, was appealingly eccentric, delightfully entertaining, and ravenously engaged in class discussions with what I later learned were classic topics in philosophy: What is it to be a virtuous person, to live "the good life," or to act in morally justified ways? What is a socially just society, and what is necessary to have one? Is there a God, and if so, can one prove God's existence? What is the mind–body problem, and how is it resolvable—that is, if it is resolvable? What is free will, and how is it reconciled with determinist accounts of human behavior? What is art, and what makes an art object beautiful?

One of the books we read in Professor Hanks' class was *Frannie and Zoey*. I remember really liking the book but liking even more Professor Hanks' classroom antics and philosophical humor when talking about *Frannie and Zoey*. It was in Professor Hanks' class that I was first introduced to what re-

mains one of my favorite philosophical texts, Bertrand Russell's *The Problems of Philosophy*, particularly the final chapter, "The Value of Philosophy."

What makes Professor Hanks' class memorable is not the content; I hardly remember more than I have described here. Rather, it was his uncanny ability to motivate and inspire his students to think philosophically and to apply philosophical concepts and theories to one's own life. I felt affirmed by him. The sorts of things he talked about were exactly the sorts of things I had been thinking about, but rarely expressed, since I was thirteen years old. His ability to make abstract and unfamiliar concepts pertinent to the life of an eighteen-year-old endeared me to him and to philosophy. Imagine my delight when I learned that a person could major, even earn a living, in sustained reflection about such things; what one needed was a Ph.D. in philosophy. My career plans were set.

Throughout my undergraduate education, I was fortunate to have other gentle and gifted teachers to inspire and encourage me in philosophy—philosophers like Gareth B. Matthews, S. Marc Cohen, and, during his last year of teaching, Wilfred Sellars.

Looking back, what these philosophers had that distinguished them from other teachers was their humility, good humor, and genuine curiosity and wonder about the ordinary world around them. To invoke Russell, they engaged us students in discussions of questions that "enlarge our conception of what is possible, enrich our intellectual imagination and diminish the dogmatic assurance which closes the mind against speculation." I knew it then: I wanted what they had and what they did. It simply never occurred to me at the time that anything other than hard work, a love for philosophy, and an excellent academic record would interfere with my pursuing a Ph.D. and career in philosophy.

On occasion, I have wondered whether, given what I know now about myself as a person and as a philosopher, I would choose a career in philosophy if I were eighteen again.

I am conflicted about such a thought. In key respects, I was quite a different person then. For one thing, by eighteen, I had felt the confusing social realities of one's race/ethnicity and socioeconomic status on one's social privilege, power, and prestige (although I did not yet know that the structural expression of these realities had names: racism and classism). I had experienced a range of gender expectations that were fairly commonplace for females in my socioeconomic, race, and geographic context. For example, I knew the rules (both covert and overt) for appropriate manners of speech for a girl ("Be polite," "Be nice," "Don't get angry," "Don't criticize men," "Let men do the talking," "Don't talk about politics or religion"), how girls should dress ("Be feminine," "Look pretty," "Wear skirts, not pants"), how girls should behave around men ("Never let a man think you are smarter than he is," "Always let the man win in games and sports," "Always smile and try to look your best"), and what constituted appropriate courses for a girl (in high school I was required to take "home economics" but prohibited from taking "shop"). I also knew that girls could be taken advantage of by boys, experience "bad touch," and "get bad reputations if they went too far." I had experienced these gender rules and expectations along with every female of my generation (although, as with racism and classism, I did not know that such expectations also had a name: sexism). But the one thing I did *not* experience as a female, living in the familial, socioeconomic, racial, and geographic context I did, was any limitation on my ability and desire to pursue a Ph.D. In fact, pursuit of a college and a graduate degree was expected. It was not until graduate school that I felt singled out as a woman, targeted for experiences that had nothing to do with who I was or what I was capable of academically. The common cultural expectations of females with which I had grown up simply did not prepare me for the sort of sexism that would await me as I began my graduate studies and career in philosophy.

For another thing, I did not know in 1965 (when I began college) that what was meant by "philosophy" and what constituted a "career in philosophy" could be significantly affected by one's gender. It was not until graduate school that I began to experience the debilitating effects of the so-called "gender neutrality" in the conception and practice of philosophy.

So, knowing what I know now, if I were eighteen again and anticipating a career in philosophy, it would be a dramatically different eighteen-year-old choosing a career that falls under a very different description of "philosophy" than the naïve one I pursued at eighteen. Sexism in the profession probably would not be something I would have to discover virtually alone—on my own, with little knowledge or collegial support to guide me.

However, what I am *not* conflicted about is what kept me in philosophy as a profession all these years. It was feminism. Without feminism, I doubt that I would have been able to overcome the sexist challenges that met me when I entered graduate school and that followed me much of my professional life. Unquestionably, it was feminism and feminist philosophy that enabled me to persevere and gradually rediscover the sense of wonder and yearning I first knew in Professor Hanks' class in 1965. The feminist reconceptualization of philosophy and philosophical methodology, its recasting of what counts as a philosophical problem, and its reframing of philosophical questions to take account of gender, race and ethnicity, class, and affectional orientation have nourished and at times sustained me ever since I "discovered" sexism during my first year of graduate school. Had I not been able to do philosophy as a feminist, I doubt that I would have continued to do it at all.

So, how did I get to that point? How did I get from the eighteen-year-old who really loved the study of philosophy to someone who struggled to maintain her commitment to a career as a professional philosopher? And how did I get from there to the rediscovery of the joys of philosophical reflection as a middle-aged adult?

I suspect my answer—my professional story—is not unique. Rather than offering here an impersonal explanation and defense of the various ways women over fifty like myself (or, as some would put it, "women before affirmative action") were subject to a variety of sexist practices, policies, and institutions in graduate school and the profession, I will simply recount some of my experiences. The examples I offer are not the worst I experienced, and they are not by themselves the basis for any reliable generalizations about the treatment of women philosophers who are now over fifty. But they are examples of the kinds of sexist treatment I experienced as a graduate student and professional philosopher, and the profound effect these experiences had on my personal and professional development. They also are examples I am willing to tell; some of the others are simply too painful and risky to write about publicly.

What were some of these formative experiences? There were those shaped by the frequent political maneuverings to undermine my credibility and effectiveness by males in positions of authority. For example, as a fourth-year graduate student who had a written contract specifying my status and salary as a now senior-level teaching associate (a graduate student teaching her own classes), I arrived at school one morning to find that, without any conversation with me, my salary had been cut roughly in half, with the difference already promised in writing to several new, first-year female graduate students. Although my position and salary were reinstated after significant protest on my part, the "divide and conquer strategy" had successfully ensured that the new female students would be angry with me for "taking away their money." I lost any chance of any female friendships or camaraderie before I had even met the new women graduate students.

There were also those shaped by the numerous not-very-funny but frequent acts of unkindness (intentional or otherwise) toward me personally by fellow graduate students and some faculty. For example, on one occasion, three male graduate students prevented me from occupying an office to which I had been assigned by making sure that the three desks, chairs, and bookcases in the office were taken—by them. One of them had even typed their three names in alphabetical order on the exterior of the office door within hours of the announcement of office assignments. They had effectively declared the office as solely and entirely theirs. When I objected by writing over their neatly typed names "I, too, occupy this office" and signing my name, one popular male faculty member wrote over my protest message, in big red scroll, "So what? Who cares!" I brought the incident to the attention of the department chair, who then asked the offending male students to apologize to me (though not to also relinquish one space so that I could have the office assigned to me). Only one of the three ever attempted to do so.

But when he did, what he said just added insult to injury: "I'm sorry for what we did, but you're right. We don't take you seriously. After all, you are never going to have to support yourself and your family the way we do." (For the record, I never did get the office spot and have been sole or primary support for myself and my daughter for nearly twenty-five years.)

There were also the behaviors in the classes themselves that marginalized me. In some classes (there were exceptions), my presence was rarely acknowledged. When I raised my hand, I was seldom called on. Note taking in these classes took relatively little time, and I grew increasingly frustrated by the inability to be recognized as a contributing member of class discussions. Since my upbringing in a New England, WASP (white Anglo-Saxon Protestant) family, I had been inculcated with the work ethic and its values of not wasting time and of being productive; therefore, I took to crocheting afghans in these classes. By the end of three years of graduate school classes, I found I had produced nine double-bed-size afghans. They made wonderful Christmas presents for members of my family.

Structural features of the department also often contributed to my isolation. For one thing, there were few women graduate students in my department. I was one of only two full-time, predissertation-stage women graduate students throughout the three-year period during which graduate students took courses. The other female student was struggling to stay alive as well. Thankfully, we became best friends in graduate school and commiserated daily.

For another thing, this philosophy department was large, with only one woman faculty member. As I remember it, this woman had full-time status in the department but taught half of her courses through the university's residential-life program, in dormitory settings. I don't presume to know this well-known feminist philosopher's story, but I do know what I witnessed. A variety of overt and covert behaviors were targeted toward her that were intended to ostracize her and, had many of them had their way, "run her out of the department." The message to me and other graduate students was clear: stay away from her, her classes, and her philosophical perspectives.

Certain behaviors and practices excluded me outside of class as well. (This point is important, since most of a student's time is spent outside of class.) I learned quickly that I was not welcome at times when and in places where my (male) peers "talked philosophy": during men-only luncheons or men-only study sessions; during men-only basketball games and other men-only sports-related environments. When I asked whether I could join them on the basketball court, I was effectively silenced by smirks. Rather than fight it, I withdrew.

These in-class and outside-of-class behaviors toward me meant that my philosophical skills and expertise were routinely discounted. For instance, to my knowledge, I was one of only two graduate students in my class awarded full teaching assistantships upon entering graduate school. I was the only graduate student to receive all A's during the three years of course work, and I was the only graduate student voted the best teacher in the philosophy department (faculty and graduate students included). Yet it was not unusual for some peers and faculty to make such comments as "You are a good teacher only because you are very motherly to your students," "You only get good grades because you are a hard worker and overachiever," and (from a department chair) "People around here don't like you very much because you smile too much, especially early in the morning."

Another example of the discounting of my abilities had significant consequences for my job prospects. When I was a finalist at a school where I really wanted to teach, I learned that my department's job-placement director had, without my knowledge, called the search-committee chair at that school and told him that I really wasn't very good. He then offered in my place a "superior [male] candidate." I learned about all of this from the chair of the search committee himself. He phoned to tell me what the faculty member (job-placement officer) in my department had said about me; he then added that he was sorry, but he was just too afraid to take a chance on me, given all that my department's placement officer had said. A bit later, I also learned that the same faculty member had not put my name forward for *any* of the colleges or universities with advertised positions. I realized then that as long as this system for placing graduate students was in place, I would only get job interviews if I went around the system: that is, needed to apply for jobs on my own and not tell anyone, especially the faculty member responsible for job placements, where I was applying or being interviewed. The year I did that, I had three job offers.

I think the final coup d'état for me as a graduate student occurred when I began writing my doctoral dissertation. I had completed writing nearly one hundred pages on section 2 of Leibniz's *The Monadology*: "And there must be simple substances because there are composites; for the composite is only a collection or *aggregatum* of simple substances." But the more I worked on the dissertation, the more I felt disingenuous about myself as a person and philosopher. The thought that persistently emerged was this: "Who besides Leibniz scholars could possibly care about this? The truth is, I don't even care about this anymore!" As was the battle cry of the late 1960s and early 1970s, I wanted to write on something "relevant." This serious confrontation with myself was a pivotal moment in my personal and professional development. It resulted in my writing a dissertation on a topic I thought was both philosophically and practically important, even though it meant that I would lose whatever credibility I still had among most members of the department. To this date, I have never regretted the decision.

Drawing on my love of the outdoors and my interest in law, I abandoned the dissertation on Leibniz in 1974 and instead began to explore what would now be called "environmental ethics" or "environmental philosophy." I sought a philosophically rich legal case to explore as a dissertation topic. Ultimately, I settled on *Sierra Club v. Morton*, which led me to Christopher Stone's *Should Trees Have Standing: Toward Legal Rights for Natural Objects*. Fascinated by the philosophically provocative but underdeveloped text and footnotes of Stone's groundbreaking book, I decided to try to answer a single question: Is there any aspect of the United States legal tradition that would prevent the meaningful ascription of legal rights to nonhuman natural objects? To that end, I immersed myself in the study of jurisprudence for two years. I then began my dissertation. In it, I argued that the answer to the question I had posed was "No": appeal to the United States legal tradition, whether understood as a natural law, legal positivist, or sociological jurisprudence tradition, provided no good philosophical grounds for rejecting the view that legal objects could be granted legal standing to sue for their own preservation. I finished the dissertation and graduated with a Ph.D. in philosophy in 1978 (eight years after I had entered graduate school).

Not surprising, my dissertation was not very good. Here I was, a female graduate student trained in the analytical tradition, in whom my institution had invested a great deal of money but little mentoring, writing a dissertation on legal rights for trees! Finding helpful, supportive, knowledgeable members for my dissertation committee was not easy. Nor was the effort of tackling a new field in a creative way, since most of my graduate training had been in critiquing *other* philosophical essays through the use of counterexample and "logic chopping." These skills served me well in graduate school, where the focus was on refuting, "tearing apart," or "destroying" someone else's argument. But they were ill suited to the task of creating one's own novel or original argument virtually from scratch (that is, where there was virtually no available secondary literature). As a result, my dissertation reflects the limitations of what one female graduate student in the mid-1970s, on her own, with little professional input or support, doing something virtually brand-new in philosophy, could produce.

For my graduate school department, however, my dissertation was more than that. It was crowning evidence that my commitment to philosophy was seriously lacking and that my future as a philosopher was bleak. The most common response to my choice of dissertation topics was like the response to my starting a high school philosophy program in 1972 (what I have since been told was the second such program in the United States): that I simply did not understand what philosophy was and that I never would be a very good philosopher. I imagine that for some, it was as if I had deliberately set out to insult them, my department, and the profession of philosophy by writing such a dissertation.

Given this history, receiving a Ph.D. in philosophy has always felt to me more like a psychological and sociological accomplishment than a philosophical one. Bottom line, what made it happen was my stubborn persistence and determination. My experience was something like that of the last survivor on the island: I made it, but with a lot of challenges, interference, and ill will from people who were supposed to help me.

During my early beginnings as a graduate student, I did not realize that the kinds of treatment I received had a name: sexism. I began to learn that much of what was happening to me was about me as a woman (not as a person or a philosopher) and that it was caused by overt and covert sexism at both personal and institutional levels. I also began to understand that what was happening to me was not my fault, that I was not merely an overachiever, and that my interests in philosophical aspects of environmental issues and philosophy for children were legitimate philosophical concerns. But the newness of this awareness, coupled with the lack of any meaningful support system for me personally or for my philosophical interests, meant that I had not yet changed my feelings of inadequacy. Like many professional women of my generation, I continued to internalize the exclusion, marginalization, and put-downs with such self-talk as "I just am not smart enough," "I only get good grades because I work so hard, not because I am any good at philosophy," and "People don't like me because there is something wrong with me." One of my coping strategies was to go home at night, put on a Holly Near album, and at full volume, sing along with her as she sang about feelings and events I was experiencing. The internal changes, indeed, the *transformation* that feminism provided me, would come later—much later.

It has been nearly twenty-five years since I received my Ph.D. Since then, even as an accomplished professional philosopher, I have continued to experience sexism and sexual harassment—a particular kind of power that "Ups" exercise over "Downs" in unjustified "Up–Down" systems of domination. (Instances of sexual harassment, as well as verbal and physical threats to my person, are among the examples I will not discuss here.)

I have had struggles around publishing that had nothing to do with the merits of my article. For example, an editor refused to publish an article that had received glowing blind reviews on the grounds that it had a story in it. The editor's worry was that publishing a story would leave the journal vulnerable to lots of people sending their favorite nature stories, thereby impugning the integrity of the journal. Ultimately, the issues were negotiated, and a revised version of the original submission was published. Paradoxically and unfortunately for me, some of the published criticisms of that essay are directed at parts of the essay that were *not* in the original essay, but were made in order to get the negotiated essay published.

Challenges have also been made to my status as a philosopher, insofar as I was a feminist philosopher. I have been told, "Philosophy is objective and impartial. Feminism is political. So, it's an oxymoron to be a feminist philosopher." I have been asked, "Why do you have to call yourself a feminist philosopher? Why can't you just be a philosopher like everyone else?" In one case, I stumbled into an informal gathering of philosophers where a colleague was holding up an anthology on ecofeminism I had just published and said (not knowing I was there), "Can you believe she gets away with this shit?"

A particularly poignant case of discounting my status as a philosopher (insofar as I taught feminist philosophy) concerns an outside review of my department. The reviewers' final report to my department and institution included this observation and recommendation:

> Karen Warren is in considerable demand by the new Gender Studies Program, and there is also a strong call for her departmental courses on feminist issues. Her training and interests would lead her to teach courses on historical figures like Descartes and Leibniz and on logic, as well; she should be strongly encouraged to do so, for the sake of her own professional development as well as for the strength she can bring to the departmental curriculum. Nonetheless, she should for most purposes be considered to be only half-time in the department, since the need for her in Gender Studies is not likely to diminish.
>
> This means that even with a new appointment there will be only three and one half persons teaching philosophy at [my institution].

According to this external review, my department had only three and one-half full-time philosophers (rather than four, as I had always thought) since according to the reviewers, my courses in feminism did not count as philosophy courses. The message to me, my colleagues, and my college's administration was clear: Although I had a full-time appointment in the philosophy department, I was really only functioning as a half-time member, which was because the feminist courses I taught in Gender Studies (or, to put it more accurately, the feminist philosophy courses I taught that happened to be cross-listed in Gender Studies) disqualified me as a philosopher. From the perspective of the outside reviewers, to "be a feminist philosopher" is an obvious oxymoron (i.e., one patently self-contradictory—a position taken to deserve neither further elaboration nor justification).

I have experienced mere dismissals of, or nonengagement with, myself and what I have had to say to the extent that what I had to say was grounded in personal experience. On one occasion in a public venue, a male philosopher was profoundly struck by my passion and comments about sexism in the conception and practice of philosophy. At the first break in the session, he approached me with visible hurriedness, the pallor of his face and mild shock at what I had said apparent in his gait and demeanor. Looking at me rather dumbfoundedly, he asked, with a mixture of surprise and confusion in his voice, "How do you *know* all that? Where did you learn it? Did you read it in some book?" I wanted to be politic and polite in my answer. Perhaps I was. All I could think to say was "No, I didn't learn it in a book. I've lived it." He stared at me for a few seconds and then simply walked away. I guess he thought that if the source of my comments was based on my felt, lived experience rather than on some text in a book, neither my comments nor continued dialogue with me about them warranted a response—personal or philosophical.

I have also had challenges to my status and authority as a professor, especially when I first began teaching as a Ph.D. Apparently, I looked quite young and was often mistaken for a student. My age and appearance seemed to confound some male students, particularly those who were within ten years of my age. They would ask me how they should refer to me. "Do you want to be called Professor Warren or Dr. Warren or Karen?" Typically, I would say that referring to me by my first name was fine, but there were the occasional male students who called me "sweetie" or put their arm around my shoulder when talking to me. For them, I asked that they call me "Dr. Warren" or "Professor Warren." That select group included the male student who, in the middle of a class, asked me, "Do you shave your legs?"

I was trained as an analytical philosopher in the logical positivist tradition. I had been taught and accepted the prevailing worldview: philosophy is the pursuit of Truth; a human being is an atomistic, autonomous, rational agent (or, rational self-interested pleasure maximizer); the moral (and scientific) point of view is that of the detached, disinterested, objective observer; there are objective, universal, cross-culturally valid principles (whether ethical, epistemological, metaphysical, logical, or scientific principles); logic and logical analysis provide the best, perhaps only, way to arrive at these fundamental Truths and principles; and the primary job of the philosopher is to find and defend these Truths and principles. Everything I had studied and read as part of my formal training in philosophy reaffirmed this worldview.

But as my personal and professional life became increasingly more disrupted and problematized by the various forms of sexism and lack of collegiality I experienced, I found it increasingly more difficult to separate off my experiences from the subject matter I studied. To borrow an expression from Naomi Scheman, I found it difficult "to push away the world." The philosophical worldview I had been taught and had accepted began to unravel. This time was not a pleasant one in my life. Everything I had believed and taught about philosophy seemed uncertain, if not patently false. In order to maintain my own integrity and sense of my self, I had no choice but to challenge it.

Mainstream philosophical discussions of the mind–body provide a case in point. In discussions of contemporary versions of, and responses to, the mind–body problem, I found it painfully unsettling to think of myself as an atomistic, disembodied Cartesian ego, or a mere material being, or a rationally self-interested pleasure maximizer. My felt, lived, and at times problematic physicality as both a woman and mother simply did not fit any time-honored story of the self I knew. At first, this conflict between standard philosophical views of the self that I had inherited and the one I was living was alternatively a source of confusion, anger, and shame. What remained constant was the felt conflict between my sense of myself as a subject—as a woman and mother and philosopher—and my experiences of being perceived as an object by others.

One particular example of this conflict stands out for me. Not long after I began my first academic appointment, my department and another philosophy department spent the weekend together on a philosophical retreat at a relatively remote cabin. The purpose of the retreat was for all of us present to engage in philosophical conversation with a preeminent philosopher about his latest book. I had not known about this retreat when the school year began. At the time, I had an eight-month-old daughter whom I was nursing. (My nursing her was her only source of food.) Being away from her for an entire weekend without much advance notice caused significant problems for both of us. For me, the problems were physically painful and embarrassing: My motherhood, particularly my condition as a lactating mother—two traits that I shared with no one else at the retreat—required that I excuse myself often from the philosophical conversations of the group. One thing that made this experience particularly difficult for me was that my discomfort was unavoidably public. There are only so many ways a nursing mother can cope with lactation in a small cabin with nearly all men and very little privacy! Another was that it was painfully obvious to me that none of the men present had ever had to think about their "home life" when planning a retreat (or, for that matter, when attending an American Philosophical Association meeting). They did not conceive of themselves as men or male philosophers doing their job; they were just philosophers doing their job. In contrast, my worldview was that I was a mother and woman philosopher; this view was in direct conflict with their (presumed) gender-neutral conception of philosophers.

There also have been challenges associated with my chosen area of scholarly focus and expertise: ecofeminist philosophy. Although this area is one in which I have had the most visible impact on the field of philosophy, it, too, has often been a source of derision and exclusion for me, including among feminists philosophers. Consider how one well-known feminist philosopher recently introduced me to a nationally renowned guest speaker at a formal dinner: "I want you to meet Karen Warren. She is an ecofeminist, but the good kind. She doesn't do that Goddess shit." For me, that was a conversation stopper. I just smiled and said, "I am delighted to meet you."

Because I am proud of my role in helping to create and foster ecofeminist philosophy, it is at times difficult to accept that, by and large, ecofeminist philosophy has yet to find the place and recognition it deserves in feminist philosophy. In my scholarship, I have rigorously argued for the importance of ecofeminist insights into analyses of and solutions to the domination and exploitation of women. In particular, I have argued that feminism is about gender, race, socioeconomic status, and geographic location (among other things); therefore, it should take seriously ecofeminist philosophical insights into the interconnections—historical, socioeconomic, conceptual, symbolic, linguistic, religious, political, ethical, epistemological, scientific—among human systems of domination and exploitation of other humans (especially women), and human systems of domination and exploitation of nonhuman animals and the Earth. I have painstakingly attempted to identify, analyze, and consider the implications of these interconnections. But, at present, I can only look forward to the day when other feminist philosophers recognize the respects in which nonhuman animals and nature are feminist issues.

Of course, not all my experiences as a graduate student or professor have been negative. I continue to enjoy teaching, developing innovative uses of electronic technologies in my courses, and engaging in philosophical conversation with my students. Several of these students have gone on to pursue Ph.D.'s in philosophy, women's studies, or feminist studies. Others have pursued careers in public service, grassroots organizing, and social-justice work. Many continue to play important roles in my life. I know from what they do and what they say to me that my teaching and scholarship has made a positive difference in their lives.

I have also come to thoroughly enjoy writing and publishing. I have been fortunate to have edited the first anthologies in ecofeminist philosophy. I am gratified by the attention my twelve-year book project, *Ecofeminist Philosophy: A Western Perspective on What It Is and Why It Matters*, has received. My current book project, *Gendering Western Philosophy: Pairing Men and Women Philosophers from the 5th Century* B.C.E. *to the Present*, takes me back to my roots and training in the history of philosophy, but with a distinctive feminist twist. This anthology will ensure that any philosopher who teaches the history of (Western) philosophy will now have a text of (and no excuse for not teaching) women philosophers alongside their male philosopher contemporaries.

In some deep Socratic sense, where public philosophy is an honorable profession, I have also loved the philosophical work I have done over the last thirty years in nonacademic contexts: teaching philosophy to elementary school children and their teachers; conducting critical-thinking workshops for nonprofit organizations; facilitating environmental ethics workshops in churches and synagogues, nature centers, science museums, and bookstores; teaching in and now directing a summer college preparatory program for local students of color entering the eleventh and twelfth grades; facilitating a "women's issues" book club at a local booksellers. And wonderful opportunities lie ahead, such as serving as a member of the Philosopher's Committee (chaired by Martha Nussbaum). Our main goal will be to have various countries of the world declare the great apes a World Heritage Species and to write (international) legislation that will ensure their survival and the survival of their habitats. It is through these activities as a public philosopher that I am philosophically most alive and most directly able to satisfy my long-standing need to make philosophy "relevant."

My love of things philosophical started early on in my life. It got a name and focus during those few months in Professor Hanks' introductory philosophy class. It grew and took form as an undergraduate philosophy major. It was not until I was a Ph.D. student and then a professional philosopher that sexism challenged some of my most basic views of myself as a person, student, and philosopher.

But that was then, and this is now. What made possible my continued commitment to things philosophical and the confidence I have now as a professional philosopher was feminism. Feminism is what helped me make sense of what was happening to me during and since graduate school; it has helped me affirm the experiences I had as a woman (rather than as a philosopher or person per se); and it has helped me begin to articulate a conception of myself and selves that is not only gendered, but also raced, socioeconomically situated, affectionally oriented, and geographically and historically located.

In the here and now, I am a woman who is a feminist, an ecofeminist philosopher, and a feminist philosopher. And I am delighted to be here.

About the Contributors

Linda Martín Alcoff is Professor of Philosophy, Political Science, and Women's Studies at Syracuse University. Her books include *Feminist Epistemologies*, coedited with Elizabeth Potter (1993); *Real Knowing: New Versions of the Coherence Theory* (1996); *Epistemology: The Big Questions* (1998); *Thinking from the Underside of History,* coedited with Eduardo Mendieta (2000); and *Identities: Race, Class, Gender, and Nationality,* coedited with Eduardo Mendieta (2003). The title of her forthcoming book is *Visible Identities: Race, Gender, and the Self.* She has written over sixty articles on topics concerning epistemology, sexual violence, the politics of knowledge, and gender and race identity.

Sandra Lee Bartky is Professor of Philosophy and Gender and Women's Studies at the University of Illinois, Chicago. Her interests include feminist theory, critical theory, critical race studies, phenomenology, Marxism, and psychoanalysis. She is a founder of the Society for Women in Philosophy, now an international network. Her publications include *Femininity and Domination: Studies in the Phenomenology of Oppression* (1991) and *Sympathy and Solidarity and Other Essays* (2002).

Teresa Brennan was the Schmidt Distinguished Professor of Humanities at Florida Atlantic University, where she was a founder of the innovative Ph.D. program in comparative studies for public intellectuals. A social philosopher with a doctorate from Cambridge University, she was a visiting professor at Harvard, Brandeis, and Cornell universities, the New School of Social Research, and the universities of London and Melbourne, among other institutions. She also served as an invited philosopher to the United Nations World

Health Organization's working group on genetic engineering and to UN presummit meetings on development. Her books include *History after Lacan* (1993); *The Interpretation of the Flesh: Freud's Theory of Femininity* (1992); *Exhausting Modernity: Grounds for a New Economy* (2000); and *Globalization and Its Terrors* (2003). Her book *Transmission of Affect* will be published posthumously.

Claudia Card is Emma Goldman Professor of Philosophy at the University of Wisconsin, with teaching affiliations in Jewish Studies, Environmental Studies, and Women's Studies. She is the author of *The Atrocity Paradigm: A Theory of Evil* (2002); *The Unnatural Lottery: Character and Moral Luck* (1996); and *Lesbian Choices* (1995). She is also editor of *The Cambridge Companion to Simone de Beauvoir* (2003), *On Feminist Ethics and Politics* (1999), *Adventures in Lesbian Philosophy* (1994), and *Feminist Ethics* (1991). She is currently a senior member at the Institute for Research in the Humanities (Madison, Wisconsin), where she is at work on two books, one on responding to atrocities, the other an introduction to feminist philosophy.

Virginia Held is Distinguished Professor of Philosophy at the City University of New York. She was president of the Eastern Division of the American Philosophical Association for 2001–2002. Among her books are *The Public Interest and Individual Interests* (1970); *Rights and Goods: Justifying Social Action* (1984); *Feminist Morality: Transforming Culture, Society, and Politics* (1993); the edited collections *Property, Profits, and Economic Justice* (1980); *Justice and Care: Essential Readings in Feminist Ethics* (1995); and the coedited collections *Philosophy and Political Action* (1972); and *Philosophy, Morality, and International Affairs* (1974). She has been a fellow at the Center for Advanced Study in the Behavioral Sciences, and she has also had Fulbright and Rockefeller fellowships. She has been on the editorial boards of many journals in the areas of philosophy and political theory and has had visiting appointments at Yale, Dartmouth, UCLA, and Hamilton. She is currently working on the topics of group responsibility, terrorism, and the ethics of care.

Alison M. Jaggar is Professor of Philosophy and Women's Studies at the University of Colorado, Boulder. She teaches classes in moral and political philosophy with an emphasis on feminism, feminist methodology, feminist practical ethics, and values and social policy. Jaggar's books include *Feminist Frameworks*, edited with Paula Rothenberg (1978); *Feminist Politics and Human Nature* (1983); *Gender/Body/Knowledge: Feminist Reconstructions of Being and Knowing*, edited with Susan R. Bordo (1989); *Living with Contradictions: Controversies in Feminist Social Ethics* (1994); *Morality and Social Justice*, authored with James P. Sterba and others (1995); *A Companion to Feminist Philosophy, (Blackwell),* edited with Iris M. Young (1998).

Professor Jaggar has received numerous grants and fellowships, including a Rockefeller Foundation Fellowship and two fellowships from the National Endowment for the Humanities. Currently, she is working on a book on feminist discourse ethics, tentatively entitled, *Sex, Truth, and Power: A Feminist Theory of Moral Reason*. She is also interested in the issues raised for moral and political theory by the integration of the global economy.

Stephanie R. Lewis is managing director at Municipal Capital Management, LLC. The firm provides financial advisory services to towns and public agencies. The core of the business is in matters of planning for and financing projects such as a relief interceptor for an overloaded storm-water collection system, curing inflow and infiltration into a hundred-year-old wastewater collection system, and adding to and renovating a fifty-year-old elementary school building. She has been in this business for nearly twenty years, and she qualified for it with an MBA in finance from the Wharton School of the University of Pennsylvania. She is nonetheless a philosopher by training and inclination. She majored in philosophy at Harvard, graduating in 1966, and was a graduate student in philosophy at UCLA from 1966 to 1970. During the 1970s, she held for one year (or less) full- and part-time jobs in philosophy at Drew University, the University of Pennsylvania, Trenton State College, Rutgers University, and, three different times, at Princeton University. She has been a member of the APA since 1968. She has served on several APA committees, and she has also served for three terms as the chair of the APA's committee on nonacademic careers. She presently sits on the chair's counsel of the Board of Officers of the APA in her capacity as treasurer.

Uma Narayan received her Ph.D. in philosophy from Rutgers University in 1990. She is currently Associate Professor of Philosophy and the Director of the Women's Studies Program at Vassar College. She is the author of *Dislocating Cultures: Identities, Traditions, and Third-World Feminism* (1997). She has coedited *Reconstructing Political Theory: Feminist Perspectives* (1997) with Mary Lyndon Shanley; *Having and Raising Children: Unconventional Families, Hard Choices, and the Social Good* (1999) with Julia J. Bartkowiak; and *Decentering the Center: Philosophy for a Multicultural, Postcolonial, and Feminist World* (2000) with Sandra Harding.

Martha C. Nussbaum is Ernst Freund Distinguished Service Professor of Law and Ethics at the University of Chicago, appointed in the Philosophy Department, Law School, and Divinity School. She is an associate in the Classics Department, an affiliate of the Committee on Southern Asian Studies, a board member of the Human Rights Program, and the coordinator of the Center for Comparative Constitutionalism. Her most recent books are *Women and Human Development: The Capabilities Approach* (2000), and *Upheavals of*

Thought: The Intelligence of Emotions (2001). She was president of the Central Division of the American Philosophical Association in 1999–2000.

Andrea Nye grew up outside of Philadelphia. After elementary school, where her teachers diagnosed her as an underachiever, her upwardly mobile parents dispatched her to one of the private girls' schools recommended as suitable preparation for a companionate marriage to a successful husband. Graduating with honors, she moved on to Radcliffe College, where she took an undergraduate degree. After eight years of marriage and four children, she returned to graduate school for her Ph.D. in philosophy. For the next twenty years, she taught philosophy and feminist theory at the University of Wisconsin, Whitewater, a small college town in the rural Midwest. She is now retired, lives in Boston, and devotes her time to writing, to the stewardship of family property in Vermont, and to her granddaughters, Sophia and Amina. She is the author of many books and articles exploring the intellectual dilemmas that result when feminist theorists confront philosophical tradition. Some of her most recent books include *The Princess and the Philosopher: Letters of Elisabeth of the Palatine to René Descartes* (1999) and *Feminism and Modern Philosophy: An Introduction.*

Ofelia Schutte is Professor of Women's Studies and Philosophy at the University of South Florida. Her areas of teaching and research are feminist theory, Latin American feminisms, philosophy of culture, and continental philosophy. She is the author of *Beyond Nihilism: Nietzsche Without Masks* (1984) and *Cultural Identity and Social Liberation in Latin American Thought* (1993) as well as numerous articles and essays on feminist, Latin American, and continental philosophy. A former Fulbright scholar to Mexico and Bunting fellow at Radcliffe, she serves on the board of the feminist journal *Hypatia*. Her current interests include feminist ethics and postcolonial feminisms.

Kristin Shrader-Frechette is the O'Neill Professor of Philosophy and Concurrent Professor of Biological Sciences at the University of Notre Dame. Working in philosophy of science and in normative ethics, she is author of fourteen books and several hundred scholarly articles that have appeared in journals such as *BioScience, Science, Philosophy of Science, Ethics,* and *Journal of Philosophy*. She has been the first female president of three professional societies: the International Society for Environmental Ethics, the Society for Philosophy and Technology, and the Risk Analysis and Policy Association. Her articles and books have been translated into eleven languages, and the latest is *Environmental Justice: Creating Equality, Reclaiming Democracy* (2002). Running a pro bono center to work with minority and poor people who are victims of environmental injustice, she and her students help to show how flawed science is often responsible for siting decisions that unfairly inflict risk on poor people and minorities. Her website is www.nd.edu/~kshrader.

Karen J. Warren is Professor of Philosophy at Macalester College in St. Paul, Minnesota. Her primary areas of scholarly interest are ecofeminist philosophy, critical thinking, and, most recently, the history of Western women philosopers. She is an internationally renowned scholar who has published six books, including her most recent *Ecofeminist Philosophy: A Western Perspective on What It Is and Why It Matters* (2000). She has also published over fifty articles and given more than two hundred presentations at conferences in such places as Buenos Aires, Gothenburg (Sweden), Helsinki, Oslo, Manitoba, Melbourne, Moscow, Perth (Australia), Rio de Janeiro, and San Jose (Costa Rica), as well as throughout the United States. She is currently editing an anthology of men and women philosophers since 500 B.C.E. entitled *Gendering Western Philosophy*.

In addition to her college and university teaching, Warren has taught in a prison, and for thirty years, she taught philosophy to school children (grades one through twelve), precollege teachers, school administrators, and parents. She is Faculty Director of MACCESS, a Macalester College program for college-bound local students of color entering the eleventh and twelfth grades. Warren has received several awards for her teaching: the Macalester College Educator of the Year Award (2000) and the Teaching Excellence Award (1996); commendation for excellence in teaching by the American Philosophical Association (1997); and the first-place Gold Hugo Award from INTERCOM (International Communications Film and Video Festival) for her video "Thinking Out Loud: Teaching Critical-Thinking Skills" (1994). She received the Feminist Teacher Award (1998) for her essay "Rewriting the Future: Challenging the Mainstream Curriculum," and she has been selected to occupy the Women's Chair in Humanistic Studies at Marquette University, 2003–2004.

In her spare time, Warren loves to garden, swim, play bridge, draw, read mysteries, travel, and enjoy quiet time with her feline companion, Dugan.